T0209359

Contrast Between
Earthly Kingdom the
and the
Heavenly Kingdom

ARTHUR CHINGWARU

WESTBOW
PRESS®
A DIVISION OF THOMAS NELSON
& ZONDERVAN

This book is a work of non-fiction. Unless otherwise noted, the author and the publisher make no explicit guarantees as to the accuracy of the information contained in this book and in some cases, names of people and places have been altered to protect their privacy.

WestBow Press books may be ordered through booksellers or by contacting:

WestBow Press
A Division of Thomas Nelson & Zondervan
1663 Liberty Drive
Bloomington, IN 47403
www.westbowpress.com
844-714-3454

Scripture quotations are taken from the Holy Bible, New International Version®, NIV®. Copyright © 1973, 1978, 1984 by Biblica, Inc.™ Used by permission of Zondervan. All rights reserved worldwide.

ISBN: 979-8-3850-0682-3 (sc)
ISBN: 979-8-3850-0683-0 (hc)
ISBN: 979-8-3850-0684-7 (e)

Library of Congress Control Number: 2023916881

Print information available on the last page.

WestBow Press rev. date: 10/13/2023

28 October 2020

Contrast Between the Earthly Kingdom and the Heavenly Kingdom

The motive of this book is to search for the desire that is in people of good things to happen on earth the way they happen in heaven. There is a strong feeling in people of wanting to have something, or wishing for something to happen. People want to achieve something they long to have, through the state of mind that is expressed by wanting, wishing, longing or craving.

Contents

Introduction

It is interesting to note that sometimes we get emersed in something that we may not need to think twice about it. We may have stayed in it that we do not need to ask ourselves why we are saying it. Such as when we say, your kingdom come, we do not take time to ask why we are asking for the kingdom to come from somewhere, what has happened to the earthly kingdom?

In other words, we are saying, the earthly kingdom is corrupted so we are asking for the one that is not corrupted to come and take charge. Sometimes this kingdom we are asking for, may have come, but we do not take any notice of it and respond accordingly.

At one time people had to be reminded that the kingdom you are asking for is already here, but you are not acknowledging it. We might be excused for not acknowledging it, for the other kingdom has physical boundaries while the other is spiritual. As that is the case, then people might want to find ways of getting the two to work together, which might want the other kingdom to adapt the morality of the other, which is making it more difficult for the other, because originally, they were miles apart, of which to get them to work together could need divine intervention.

The good about it is that the one who said, it had come, did not leave it like that, but introduced the gospel, and this is inspired, it tells people about it so that no one is taken unawares.

The other one being spiritual, its spirituality can be seen in what happens in our lives When it happens, sometimes we fail to understand.

The good thing is, there are so many teachings about the two that people have got a choice of which one to pursue, we are not left in the darkness about them. This even happened before we would even ask for it, someone thought of our salvation before we would even realise it. This comes without any condition but only to have faith in Him who Loved us before we knew it, and before we loved Him.

The earthly kingdom claims to have enemies, but it is taught by the other kingdom that we do not do it that way but the way of perseverance, and the way of loving without any condition. By doing that, what we have been asking for is achievable, but there should be some sort of transformation on our part, in order to qualify for that type of life.

Even though we are trying to emulate that goodness, there are some who are showing that they do not have that brotherly love by enslaving their biological brothers just because the colour of the skin happens to be different and for the love of accumulating wealth yet the soul is created in the image of God.

It still appears that, it has not sunk in people's DNA, that the teaching of brotherhood should continue until no stone is left on top of the other. It appears the accumulation of wealth is making people to be addicted that they may not value human life. No matter how much they may try to justify it, human life should matter, and should be taken into account.

The Bible we use about human life is the same, the only difference is in the interpretation. In all this misunderstanding, the church should play a role in making people understand that there is eternity to come, which we should all strive for.

Our minds should focus on the creator who knows all our strengths and what our weaknesses are, and He knows what to do with our souls. We should bear in mind that we are working for the souls through the new covenant. This theory of wanting to get a revelation must not end with us, but passed on to the next generation.

The church teaches that we do not work for ourselves alone, but also for those who may be less privileged than us. It is not only to tell people what to do but also demonstrating by doing it ourselves. It must start with me then others will take it up. When we strive to do good, we are not alone but the Holy Spirit will guide us. The whole society will see our good works and the glory shall be to the creator, that is the goal of the church. After observing all this, then shall the end come, then that kingdom will be established here on earth.

01

The Coming
of the Kingdom

Once, on being asked by the Pharisees when the kingdom of God would come, Jesus replied. His reply was that, the kingdom of God would not come in such a way that it would be observed or neither would the people say come and see. They would not say, it is here or it is there, because the kingdom of God was in their midst, and is still in our midst, meaning that the kingdom of God is in our hearts.

(Luke 17:20-21) (NIV). We might be asking such a question today, here the answer has been given. This is not like an earthly kingdom where we say certain named kingdoms will rule a designated area, but this is a Spiritual kingdom involved in transforming people's lives. If it transforms our lives, people see it, instead, we should ask God to transform our lives first then the rest will be seen as they manifest. The kingdom of this world is rooted in wanting to see others go down only wanting itself to flourish while others are not. When we are filled with this spiritual kingdom, it means it will do away with things that are unclean and imperfect and replace them with things that are divine and of righteousness. When you pin your hopes in Him and your faith on what you have seen of His works that He showed when He came to introduce the heavenly kingdom on earth, you take note of the kingdom being on earth. The question is, whether my heart is doing what is required in order for the kingdom to manifest to the world through me? If that is not the case, then I have to ask God to transform me, my heart must yield to my Lord. After saying, your will be done in earth as it is in heaven, I must also say from the depth of my hearth that your will be done on me, that means I am humbling myself to be used as the Lord wishes. To be ruled by God is the greatest blessing a man can have, that means all your time you will be used by the Holy Spirit. This was promised by Jesus that the Holy Spirit would be with us for ever, that is why we are saying that the Holy Spirit is with us.

A Model Prayer

(Matthew 6:9-15) (NIV), is called a model prayer because it teaches Christians how they should build their lives on Jesus Christ. He did not teach them what they should do after He had gone, but He also lived that life and set an example for us to do the same. The Father is worth to be addressed like that, all Jesus is asking us to do is what He did himself. This prayer makes our relationship with God to be a strong relationship, it will be stronger because instead of us saying to God, it is your right do this to us, we are humbling ourselves and asking Him in a polite way. We are praising Him and asking Him to pardon us because what we did was not His fault, but ours. We should not be ashamed to follow His example because He is good. To be called you are like Him does not make us ashamed, let is follow Him in every step so we can be like Him in our lives. (Ephesians 5:1-2) (NIV) It is common sense that children copy their parents so it is like that to us as we should copy our Father in heaven, by doing so, we are going to be like Him, our love to our neighbours must be like the love that He showed to us. He is a model to every age like he did when He was twelve years old, He was found in the temple. It is interesting to note that the disciples continued exactly where Jesus left off and did exactly as they were taught, which means we are to take it from where the disciples left off. Christianity helps us to improve our health, because it teaches good things even to look after ourselves.

We are addressing our Father who is in heaven, this confirms our belief in Christianity that God is our Father who is in heaven, and we should maintain that relationship of Father and child. Note the collective address, we are not selfish but meaning that the Father is for us all, not trying to make Him mine alone, hallowed be your name, means His name is sanctified, His name is Holy there is no one else like Him, we must always use His name respectfully. Your kingdom come, means we are longing for the kingdom of God to take form here on earth (not a political kingdom) and let the goodness that is in heaven prevail on earth so we can live in a place that is characterised by faith and hope and love, but the greatest of them all is love, (1 Corinthians 13:13) (NIV). Love stays forever, we must also be prepared to serve others, this is so when you have faith in Him who created us. When we have that faith, that means we will keep focused on Him, faith will make us express our love to others. We are always longing for a new heaven here on earth, should this be fulfilled, we will live in a Holy City where there is no pain or death, (Revelations 21:1-4) (NIV). Although it is said the kingdom is among you, but definitely there is going to be a second coming when everything will be new, and He will establish His kingdom on earth. Then everything will be renewed, there will be no death, no pain or tears, God will wipe away all tears and we will have eternity with God the creator. Your will be done on earth as it is in heaven. This means that God reigns in heaven with compassion and justice, (Isaiah 30:18) (NIV). We have to acknowledge that love by being grateful, He is waiting to see how grateful we are to such compassionate love. We are making ourselves carry a heavy burden by only failing to acknowledge, sometimes we have pride in ourselves. If we look at all this, that means He is worthy to be praised. If we follow His example, that means we will love one another, love our neighbours as we love ourselves, this should not end on paper, but to be put into practice, (Matthew 22:37-40) (NIV). Showing no selfishness, but a total surrender to the will of God. We should pray to God to give us the strength, in our flesh, we might not be able to accomplish it.

Give us this day our daily bread, as the food nourishes the body; the good news nourishes the soul. The Bible says that man shall not live on bread alone, but with the word that comes from the mouth of the Lord, (Deuteronomy 8:3) (NIV). We pray for spiritual sustenance so that we can be able to go out into the world well-fortified, while we are there in the world, to be able to spread the word to those who are in need. Let this bread come down from heaven (John 6:48-56). When we pray, we are asking each time for our daily bread, but when Jesus says I am the bread from heaven, we fail to understand it. We should be asking for an understanding that we should be in Jesus and Him in us, then our souls are nourished.

Forgive us our debts as we forgive our debtors. This is where the prayer hinges, saying to the Lord, if I do not forgive myself, do not forgive me, if I do not sympathise with the poor do not sympathise with me. In other words, we are saying, please Lord Give me a good heart so that every good thing should start with me. When I start praying, I have to examine myself first to ensure that whatever I am asking for, I do it to others so it can be done to me as well. The reason why we want to be associated with the kingdom of heaven is that the kingdom of heaven is filled with forgiving people.

Lead us not into temptation, but deliver us from evil: Jesus was led by the Holy Spirit into the wilderness to be tempted by the devil: the Holy Spirit must enable us as it did to Jesus in the wilderness.

Pray without seizing

Later, Jesus tells his followers to pray so that they are not led into temptations as Jesus was also led into temptations. God's desire is to make us holy as He is Holy, (James 1:13) (NIV). (Matthew 6:33) (NIV)

We are told to seek first the kingdom of God and His righteousness. This means that God is pure, then, if we are seeking His righteousness, we are seeking His purity to be always like Him. We can transform the world and make it a better place to live in. The reason why we are asked to seek first His kingdom, is that there is all the goodness in his kingdom, un corrupted as the earthly kingdom. Should we be in problems, we should think of Him first because He is faithful to us to be able to take us out of those problems. As He is a caring father, we should be thinking of Him day and night. What He does, we should copy that, use it in our daily lives and it will transform us. That is not easy because there so many forces against us, they appear to be of importance in our lives yet they lead to destruction, let God rule in your life if you want to be like Him. (Romans 6:1-2) (NIV) Where we see there can be sin, we must try to avoid it, so why would we need to ask God to make us refrain from something that would make us sin. In other words, we are asking God to make us avoid the situations where we may find ourselves lured into ungodly action, (1 Corinthians 10:13) our prayer is for Him to keep us away from it altogether. Where we can avoid those situations, we should try by all means to avoid them, that is also part of our prayer, sometimes some of the suffering we may go through may produce some ungodly characters in us in the end, so we are asking God to lead us away from such things. (James 1:2-4) (NIV). The Godly character produces love peace and faith, they manifest a Christian life in us, in order to produce all that we have mentioned, we will go through hard times, but those hard times will mould us to grow in a Christian life, (Romans 5:3-5) (NIV). We know very well that we will face troubles in this world, but ask God to minimize it, since we are following in the footsteps of Jesus and emulating all that He did, in the end, we will be victorious like him, (John16:33) (NIV). Our prayer is that we submit ourselves to God's will. Trials and temptations may come, but true Christian will hold on to their faith and hold on to Jesus because He also went through them and overcame them. As followers of Christ, we will be faced with so many of these but with His grace and help we will go through like He did.

(Matthew 6:13) (NIV), in the first petition we ask for forgiveness from our past sin "forgive us our debts" asking to be forgiven from our past debts, but in this second petition, we are asking God to help us avoid future sins a potential sin before it even happens. We need to pray to be made to avoid things that might defile us in the end. We need to be delivered from all evil things in our flesh and in the world. God does not tempt anyone; He is Holy and just.

For yours is the kingdom, the Alpha and Omega of prayer must be for the glory of God. Jesus was quite clear (unequivocal) in teaching us to give (ascribe) all the glory to God. Everything must yield to the glory of God. He has supreme authority over all and unrestricted dominion over an immense empire. This is a declaration that the power belongs to God, this means that our prayer is getting to the crescendo with the announcement that all glory rightly belongs to Him.

And the power and the glory forever, for all that is in heaven and on earth, is yours. Greatness and goodness, and the beauty of God, "my glory I will not give to another, nor my praise to carved images." And the Word dwelt among us, and we beheld his glory. The reason for Him to come to dwell Among us was to show us how life should be. We pray Him to keep us from potential sins: This teaches us to humble ourselves if we want to be like Him.

The one separated from sinners, He Himself is always, Holy and harmless, to be like Him we must always be in Jesus, who is in Him. This made him of no reputation, taking the form of a bondservant, and coming in the likeness of man. He laid aside his glory and walked among us. Although He was condemned to death, killed and buried; on the third day He rose from the dead, to fulfil what He said, we must be glad that this was done for us "I am the resurrection and the life," Jesus stayed forty days after the resurrection. The reason for staying forty days after the resurrection was that he wanted to convince them beyond any doubt that He was alive. (Acts 1:9) (NIV) Jesus took His disciples out and gave them assurance that they would receive power through the Holy Spirit. As He was speaking, gradually He started being lifted up into heaven, as they looked in amazement, a cloud hid Him from their sight.

Amen, meaning certainly true, it should stay like that, verily, truly, so be it, praise be to the lord, from everlasting to everlasting.

The Contrast

The notable contrast that is there between the earthly kingdom and the heavenly kingdom is that the earthly kingdom has geographical boundaries while the heavenly kingdom is boundless. The heavenly kingdom is the work of the Spirit in a person's life or people's lives; when it transforms you, whatever you do will always reflect the kingdom of heaven, this guides us on how we are related to God for we are created in the image of God in His likeness spiritually His kingdom works through people's lives. The kingdom said to be in us is not automatic as such but depends on how we accept Him in our hearts, that is the faith we have. To understand this kingdom, we should see that people are transformed, this will happen if we ask for His revelation and His grace.

(Ephesians 6:12) (NIV) We have a very good example that Jesus was born of the Spirit but the devil could not fear that but to tempt Him, if that happened to Jesus it happens to us as well. We are fighting the forces of darkness, but the forces of darkness are not always dark, sometimes they are very shining so that we can be lured into believing that we are doing the right thing, yet in the eyes of God they lead to destruction. They are not tangible, we should not try to fight hem with tangible weapon like guns or submarine, but with spiritual weapons, underneath there is an invisible spiritual battle raging, we must not forget that they are powerful and they have got authority to rule the world. Only God can strengthen us and He makes us strong enough to be able to fight against these forces, His power can deliver us from all wickedness. These forces can even try to influence our way of thinking, once they infiltrate our way of thinking, they have won. These forces were defeated at the resurrection but they keep on trying to influence our minds that His rising from the dead was just a delusion. By the resurrection we are assured of victory, but this does not come in a plate, we have to stay vigilant for these forces are working day and night to snatch us from the salvation. God has provided us with the Holy Spirit who will always intercede for us, so when we are being tempted, we must always call on the Holy Spirit to help us.

As the kingdom of this world is dominated by the devil, it seeks to mislead people so that there is always division between God and His people. The best way to get rid of that is to stay connected to our father through prayer, but the devil seeks to disconnect all those connections. Those powers of darkness are happy to see us divided. This devil has even caused division amongst ourselves, so that there is always discord on earth, in most cases, the devil misleads by telling lies. He cannot mislead the heavenly beings because they are all divine, that is why we are asked to stay in prayer so that we stay divine as well.

02

Nature of Kingdoms

The Earthly Kingdom Carries a Sword

There are wars on earth, they say, if you want peace prepare for war, thinking that after the war there will be peace but the wars are never ending. It is better to be the one who starts to do good things to others that you should expect to get good things from them as well. How can you expect to get good things from those you are doing bad to? If you are violent to others, expect to get violence from them too or from anybody. You reap what you sow not to reap where you did not plant, it is impossible. Do not expect to get what you have not given out, always expect what you have given out. Mobsters will end up killed by their guns, so there is no point in saying that you are carrying a weapon for defence, according to Ephesians 6, there is a spiritual sword that Christians must always carry. This will help us to have a war free world which we are always asking for, we are always asking for a peaceful society full of love. There are so many reasons why there are so many wars between nations, countries, groups, families or individuals. The reason could be, economical, territorial, religious or nationalism, civil war and or political, or evolutional.

Most reasons why countries or nations or individuals fight is to increase their power, or increase their wealth. They do this by conquering or subjugating other groups or individuals and by seizing their territory and or resources. Unresolved regional tensions, breakdown in the rule of law, absence or co-opted state institutions, illicit economic gains, and the scarcity of economic gains have become the main reasons for conflict. War has a catastrophic effect on the country, groups, or individuals or nations.

When are we going to have peace? Everyone is carrying a sword for self-defence, so it never ends, compare with (Matthew 5:9) (NIV). It is a good thing to be a peace maker, blessed are the peace makers because we are all praying that there be peace on earth so that the kingdom of peace is established on earth, as it is in heaven. Jesus asked His disciples to declare peace in every home they entered because it is better to start peace, if everything follows what you started then the world will be peaceful. A peaceful world is what we are always asking for, if this happens that means His will has been done on earth as it is in heaven. The gospel that Jesus brought to this world is about peace, let this peace come from our hearts not being compelled to make peace. If we are seeking peace, it means you are seeking what the gospel stands for the gospel came for peace to every soul, in everything we do there has to be peace in order to understand each other. When we accept the gospel in our hearts it means we are accepting peace in ourselves, let it guide us, lead us, to the will of the Father who is a peace-loving Father. So, when we do our work peacefully, we are doing Him a good service that pleases Him. There is no peace in the world which means the devil is trying all it can so that there is no peace at all. We pray that it be revealed to us each time we are to fight with our brothers or sisters to think that we are fighting for the world which is not ours, we found it there and we will leave it there. The earthly kingdom practise power over their people dictating everything to its people and people having no choice but, everything is dictated to them. If you trust a sword already you have shown that you are at war and already the other side will become defensive, then you are already at war where each side wants to win the war.

The heavenly people are devoted in praising the Lord what they do, they are always in harmony to each other, they stay in peace.

As we are created in the image of God, we are really the sons of God, sometimes because of what we do, it is us who would have walked away from the Lord then we are shy to call ourselves the children or to call ourselves the sons or daughters of God. By sending His son to die for our sins was the way to consolidate that we are sons of God. This is the time that we must be working towards making peace with others which means you are looking for a peaceful world which will make our world a happy place to live in. (John 14:27) (NIV) By following Him alone shows we are making peace with Him; this is lasting peace. We must invite the Holy Spirit to be with us all the time so that what we do will be guided and we will have lasting peace in this world. When Jesus sent out His disciples, He asked them to declare peace in every house they entered (Luke 10:5-9) (NIV).

Jesus taught peace to His disciples and he expected them to be peaceful even after He left. He is well known as the prince of peace, which means if we follow Him and obey his teaching the world will be a peaceful place to live in. Jesus gave them a hint that He was sending them out as lambs among wolves, signifying what type of world we are living in. Jesus had twelve disciples but here we hear of seventy which means there were so many other than the twelve, who wanted to work for Christ, we must be in one of the seventy, working for the prince of peace.

The earthly kingdom practices power over its subjects, the way they behave is totally different from the way the heavenly kingdom behaves, the earthly kingdom thinks that if they carry a sword they are well defended and they have nothing to fear anymore. But that is not the case at all, by trusting a sword you are creating enemies for yourself. The earthly kingdom seeks to control behaviour whether you like it or not, it has got to be imposed on you. What we should take note of is that those earthly kingdoms don't last, if they seem to have lasted for some time, it is a heavy yoke on its subjects, they only survive on dictating their power over their subjects. By imposing its powers on its subjects, it creates so many enemies for itself then in the end it seeks to defend itself against the enemies it has created in the first place.

The reason why the earthly kingdom wants to carry a sword is because they want to return evil with evil. This type of life style, appears not ending soon, if there is to be any change, it may appear to be gradual not rapid as we might want it to be. We would like very much to act like Jesus, but it appears the imitation is not that very fast enough as we would like it to be.

Christians must know that theirs is the higher rule than the earthly laws, as little as our minds are, we think that justice is done when we have an eye for an eye. Yet justice is not done yet because the other side still wants to revenge, we have to be happy that we are serving the higher laws. (Exodus 21:24) This was used by judges to calculate what type of punishment that would be proportionate to the damage caused, not exactly the eye as such, but something appropriate. That is why we said, we must always ask for a revelation, because when Jesus said if someone slaps you on the cheek turn to him the other cheek, He did not literally mean turning the other check, but He meant that, do not revenge, because when revenging it does not end it keeps on and on. Even in those days, it was meant for the ease of the judges to apply a punishment that was proportionate to the damage or injury caused.

The Heavenly Kingdom Carries the Cross

Followers of the heavenly kingdom always act and behave like Jesus, because they get their example from Him, because He carried His cross to Calvary. He even said whoever wants to follow me must carry his cross and follow me. We all know what pain He went through when He was being led to Calvary after being bitten strongly and what pain He went through when He was hanging on the cross. He was saying, following He was not all that plain sailing, He was saying, when we choose to follow Him, we have chosen to go through what He went through. In the end He conquered death and rose from the dead, which means when we follow Him, we may go through some hardship, but in the end, we may also rise like He did. It appears like we hear one thing, but we do the other because it appears we are not following His footsteps. If Christians were going to follow every step as He did, surely Christians were going to transform this world. It looks like Christians are following half-heartedly. Let Christians learn to sacrifice their lives for others, it seems very impossible to follow exactly like Jesus did, but with His divine help, which we can only get if we put our trust and faith in Him that He will never forsake us. Jesus, whom we are following exercises power under other than power over, when we exercise power under, does not mean that everything is going to be plain sailing but will meet hardships along the way but to persevere unto the end like Jesus until He reached Calvary. When it is said there is power in the cross it appears very remote because there is nothing visible or something tangible. When Jesus was being led like a sheep to the cross, even His disciples deserted Him, but regrouped when He rose from the dead. This shows that even death has no power over Him, that is what Christians are being invited to do to follow Him to the end and have a resurrection of the soul in the end.

Jesus set up a very good example for us, He carried His cross to Calvary, but on the third day He rose from the dead, and has made death and evil to be powerless. He has set an example for us that we can rise again if we follow Him or if we stay connected to Him.

The Christian faith is hinged on the cross because when Jesus was carrying His cross to Calvary, He was doing it for our salvation. It is by His grace that we may get salvation, this is not by works, but by the grace. The resurrection is a pointer to us that we will also rise if we follow Him. If there was no resurrection, otherwise Christianity could be one of the social gatherings to be familiar with each other. Jesus promised beforehand that He would rise, and it happened as He had said it to prove that what He says is to be relied upon. When He says, our souls will rise again, we have to rely on that and to start expecting the resurrection of our souls when the time comes, we will expect eternal life.

Very few people are prepared to suffer in order to carry the cross, carrying the cross means going through difficult times in order for others to have a good life. Jesus did not like going through such difficult times in order for us to have salvation, He even asked why His Father had forsaken Him, in order for you and me to be saved. Carrying the cross is like planting a fruit tree, you cannot harvest it in the next short period of time, but after a long time. When Jesus carried His cross to Calvary, no one knew there could be the resurrection. He did that for you and me, are you prepared to die for your friends, because that means following Jesus' foot-steps, He even asked why His Father had forsaken Him, times were difficult. Do not expect plain sailing in a Christian life, you must be prepared to sacrifice for others, because that is the great commission in which Jesus said teach all nations, in order to have others saved. Let us pray for the Lord to change us so that we are more kind, be compassionate to others always, do not look down upon others for you do not know what the Lord thinks about them, avoid anything that could hurt others always have that feeling of helping others.

Ensure Your Name is there in the Book of Eternity

There is a book of eternity written for the saints who may be chosen for eternity. By following the requirement of Him who keeps this book of eternity, we all know the requirements, it is only that sometimes we would like to create our own book of eternity. This means we are at variance with the requirements if we are trying to create our own without following the what is originally set as the entry qualification, it is that when you were born, your name was written in the book of eternity, but as we go through the journey of life, by our deeds the name is either left permanently there or it will be blotted out, ensure it is not blotted out. It appears the condition is simple, because it is a matter of choice to either receive Him in your heart. To accept Him in your heart is to follow His example in all what He has shown us, and also go through what He went through, and in the end, you will do like He did, and now is alive.

The Kingdom of the World is Rooted in Advancing Its Own Interests

The worldly governments seem to love the people as if it was doing like the heavenly kingdom that loves the people, but the difference is that it only loves people of its own nationality or people of its own race. In such circumstances, people want to identify themselves with a certain group race or nationality, before identifying themselves as the children of the same Father. They share the same geographical area, share the same language and a common culture, share the same origin, the same ideas and the characteristics of that culture. It has individual intend to advance your own interests, and your own welfare, riches you want them to be all yours. There is a struggle between governments or between individuals because of selfishness. The kingdom of this world wants to rule over our hearts

The earthly kingdom is trying to emulate the heavenly kingdom but lacks the divinity and will start loving selectively. If we are really following the love of God, we will start loving with brotherly love taking everyone as your brother or your sister, regardless of where they come from.

On the Cross the Thief Asked to be Remembered by Jesus in His Kingdom

These words were said on the cross when one had seen the divinity of the cross. Sometimes we fail to see the connection between the cross and the kingdom, yet from the cross we are going right into the kingdom. The man on the cross did not ask for anything else, but he was specific and asked for the thing that matters. This is the time when everything is coming to an end, even Jesus is asking from His Father for what matters because we have come to a crucial stage. So, when we are facing the cross, we have no time to talk about things that do not concern eternity, we are in the dying minutes of the game, so let us choose what to carry with us to eternity. We would say the man on the cross was very blessed because He had a revelation because without a revelation you cannot see the value of things that have value, at the time when a man was being forsaken by many, was the time when one sees the glory of a man coming in clouds. In our days to choose the cross against the sword is choosing eternity. Let ask to be revealed to us what is hidden in the cross that when others see despair, I see the glory in the despair. It is not blessed to only see the immediate future and failing to see the remote future, to be able to see the importance of the cross. Sometimes when we are faced with difficult times and we pray, we expect things to easy straight away but that was not the way on the cross, there is no where we are told that Jesus eased his pain on the cross but only that he was promised that he would be with Jesus in paradise. Whenever we come to the cross, we must ask to be remembered, once we are assured, we will know that our names are there in the book of eternity

The reason why there are conflicts in the world is because of selfishness whether it be countries or whether it be individuals. When they are countries because they only regard the people of their nationality as the only people disregarding all the other nationalities as if they were not sons and daughters from the same Father, yet if it is looked at broadly, we are the same, there is no need for those conflicts.

(Revelation 11:15) (NIV) Yet when this world will be ruled by the prince of peace when the trumpet is sound and His kingdom will be established on earth He will rule with justice and all fairness and will rule for ever. No more pain, no more tears, for death and pain were defeated on the cross and at the resurrection. (Daniel 7:15-28) (NIV)

One who Carries a Sword dies of a sword

In (Luke 22:36) (NIV) Earlier on when Jesus was sending out His disciples, He instructed them not to carry any tunic or any bags of food, had also instructed that if someone hits you one the cheek, give him the other, is the same Jesus who is talking of buying swords. The words to note from Jesus were, when He said two swords were enough. In this case, Jesus meant that they should be prepared with their spiritual swords because there were hard times ahead. Jesus Himself demonstrated it, when He was being led to the cross, Jesus never took out a sword Himself, and also when He was sending them out, He ordered them not to carry a tunic, a sword or any food, also when they misunderstood Him on the sword, He said to them two swords were enough, for Jesus was trying to cut the long story short. Two swords could not be enough to defend Him when He was taken to the cross. The author is pleading with the reader, when He came onto the world means that the kingdom has already come, the kingdom of God means love, Jesus Himself means love, we must love one another because God is love. The church should always preach the love of God; thus, two swords are enough, they are enough to fulfil the prophecy. Christians must know that even if they are the followers of Christ, the temptations will always be on them, but to know that Christ will always fight for them, and will always fight our battles for us, we must feel relaxed. Where we see we can be tempted into sinning, we must try to avoid such situations before we are caught unawares by the devil who is very cunning. In Christianity we face different temptations, therefore we must be ready to defend our Christianity by all means that are possible at our disposal, this will help us in the end. We must always try to understand the scriptures in order for us not to give wrong interpretation. This was the fulfilment of prophecy Interpretation, how could Jesus instruct His disciples to buy a sword, yet when He was being led to the cross, never took out a sword Himself, He would have used His power that He would have made them to suffer bad things and Jesus would have set Himself free. Jesus was fulfilling a prophecy, look into the matter closely, His talking of two swords being enough, However, to justify the accusation that Jesus is the head *of a band of* brigands in the same way, the eternal happiness, we must expect to be assaulted and sifted by Satan. *Jesus* taught us that in all the temptations we come across, we must be on our guard through prayer for even He himself stayed in prayer and He overcame all the temptations and received glory in the end. He wants us to have faith so that we can be able to do greater things that we cannot do without faith. When we have faith in our Lord that means we will stay in good relationship with Him who loves us and wants us to have eternal life which is what we are striving for all the time. We must always be on the alert so that we are not attacked by the devil if we are not attacked that means we will stay closer to Him who loves us. If the devil fails to destroy, he will try to make some people fall from favour or to inflict pain on them. Nothing more certainly forebodes a fall, in a professed follower of Christ. See, (Matthew 26:52) (NIV): The Lord wants to manifest Himself through the church, but it appears we are taking the opposite direction since these disciples were with Jesus for three years Peter would not have taken that direction. It is looking like we are looking for a quick solution and forgetting that Jesus' solution was to go through the cross. If we are to follow Christ's example, we have to follow His example in truth and in spirit. Jesus is demonstrating to us if we want to be happy, we must start by pleasing other people to be happy because in return they will make us happy. Whatever you do to others it will be done to you as well, Jesus was saying, do not use a sword on others, for the one who uses a sword will die of a sword. Peter was asked to Put his sword back in its place, Jesus warned Peter of the dangers of using a sword because anyone who uses a sword dies of a sword. Which shows that the disciples were not meant to use it in his defence. Jesus spoke only of spiritual warfare. The sword of the spirit is the sword with which the disciples of Christ must furnish themselves. It is not likely that He would teach them to use it in their own defence, as they preached the gospel of the kingdom. Yet Jesus said to his followers that they could move mountains and tons of earth and granite with faith? In contrast, (Luke 22:51): This corrupt world will always push us to the limits, before we can realise, we have reacted to the provocation from this corrupt world, but only to regret later after we have reacted in a hush. If we would learn to let things take their course, we would be surprised to learn how things would be obeyed, I pray that we follow Jesus' example, no matter how painful it might appear, because that is the only way we can be like Christ, not in word but in deeds to live a life that we preach. Jesus told Peter not to do that anymore, and He touched a man's ear and healed him. In Matthew's account, Jesus is not taking it lightly with Peter. This will leave us with no doubt but knowing what to follow, (John 18:11) (NIV) Peter had been with Jesus for three years how he had performed his miracles telling his disciples that he would one day go. Peter heard him say He would have called ten thousand angels. For Peter to intervene in that way meant that he did not know Jesus well. Jesus asked Peter, to put his sword away, because if He had allowed what Peter had done, that would mean He was not going to drink cup His Father had given Him.

If Peter who was with Jesus daily for three years, did not understand Him, do we understand Him yet. If we do understand Him, let us keep it up, if we do not know Him yet, we should not despair, let us ask for His guidance He is faithful and honest enough to help us. In Luke 6:29) (NIV) "And to him, that smite your cheek, offer him also your other cheek, and he who takes away your coat give him your jacket as well". Jesus is not literally meaning that to someone who hits your cheek give him the other. He wanted followers who do not come to Him with some different motives, but genuine followers. When following Jesus you will meet some disappointments, but you need to focus on Christ not spending your time thinking of ways to revenge, instead of spending their time seeking salvation which is the main goal of Christianity. Followers of

Jesus must be people who are prepared to deny themselves and follow Jesus in truth and in Spirit. That is the reason why this book insists on asking for revelation because here it does not literally mean that you should turn the other cheek but that you should not retaliate or seek revenge. We can only overcome evil by doing good. (Romans 12:21) NIV) Do not be overcome by evil but to overcome evil by doing good deeds, when trying to do good it will appear you are being defeated yet even Jesus gave that example, that even His disciples were surprised, to forgive normally breaks the cycle of retaliation and leads to an understanding of each other and start building a relationship.

Our worldly possessions are temporal, they must not be barriers that may hinder us from entering the kingdom of God. We need to be reminded time and again that we are only stewards of these things, because when it comes to the time of going, we will leave them all here and go without them. Let us seek for spiritual things that will have eternal life, so that when the time comes, we are ready for something everlasting. Let us fix our eyes on something that has a future and something everlasting.

The Heavenly Kingdom Carries the Cross

As God loved the world, He gave His own Son as the saviour of the world, but he had to go via the cross. Christians must live their lives according to the will of God not as the culture tells us, in that we meet hardships which we would not have met if we were living as we wished that is why living such a life is called carrying your won cross because you are living according to the will of God when we meet hardships or persecutions, we deal with them the way Jesus dealt with them. The reason why Simon of Cyrene was chosen and forced to carry the cross was because he showed some sympathy with the way he saw Jesus' suffering, as we show sympathy with Christianity, we are also made to carry the cross as was done to Simon of Cyrene. When we choose to be the followers of Jesus, means we have chosen to be Jesus' disciple which means we have sacrificed so many earthly things in deciding to follow Jesus, that means you are carrying your own cross to Calvary as Jesus did. (Luke 9:23) (NIV) We must not be living a life of pretending and lip service and do the real discipleship life and learn to sacrifice our live for Christ because He himself did the same for us who are we to say we cannot reciprocate, let us follow Him in spirit and in truth. The power of the cross of Jesus is to reconcile us humanity with our heavenly Father. Jesus gave us a new life when He rose from the dead, which means he did that for us to also follow Him means we will also rise like Him. On the cross is where sin was defeated and his rising from the dead sealed it, this means we have been made whole by the blood of Jesus. By suffering such great pain on the cross, Jesus showed His love to us, that is why all the glory must go to Him. In Christianity sometimes we live in fear of showing our true identity, but there are times we have to be bold enough to confront those who say Christianity is bad. Joseph of Arimathea is remembered to this day, because he was a member of the Pharisees who used to despise Jesus, but in his own heart he was convicted and saw some divinity in Jesus, we may do things in a crowd, but there are times we must see the goodness in Christianity. When you are on one to one with the Lord, you must ask for some revelations, so that you can just move with the crowd, but do the will of God. Let us ask God to give some divine favours like He did to the robber who was also crucified with Jesus to be able to say Jesus remember me when you get to your kingdom. It was not easy, but it pays to know what to say at the right time, sometimes we become ashamed to say these things but we have to because they mean eternity. The story of salvation starts in a manger with the birth of Jesus Christ and ends with Jesus carrying the cross to Calvary. The cross was the climax of the story of Jesus or the story of the salvation of man. In the very beginning, Christ chose to come and suffer, sacrifice His blood, He even chose to die such death on the cross in order to save man from his sins. Salvation is the saving of human beings from sin and its consequences, we all know that the consequence of sin is separation from God resulting in death. To save ourselves from this, we have to believe in His Son Jesus Christ for He was sent here to redeem us from our sins. A man was to be made a slave of Satan forever, but Jesus decided to put that to an end by going on the cross. The story of the heavenly kingdom is redefined on the cross. The story is long, from the garden of Eden until the day of the cross when sin was defeated, but then, even now the sin wants to persist. When Jesus said, the kingdom of heaven has come; He meant to say we must try to do good all the time to everyone so that all those good works will represent what is happening in heaven, so the heavenly kingdom will be represented here on earth, it was concluded at the cross. Man was given this power to represent the heavenly kingdom, Jesus said to Peter, I give you the keys of heaven and earth. What you bind here on earth will be bound in heaven what you loosen here on earth will be loosened in heaven. This means that man was regaining that lost responsibility when he ate a fruit from a tree he was forbidden to eat. Jesus came to redefine and to make a man go back to the original. Jesus said all the powers were given to Him in heaven and on earth since He said if you do as I tell you to do, I will call you my friends, and all the power that was given to me I will give to you also. Jesus does not exploit his power as Adam did but he humbles himself a servant of all, Jesus teaches us to humble ourselves as He did so that we will be exalted in the end as He did but by doing so, he becomes an exalted ruler of all. (Philippians 2:5-11) (NIV). If we are pursuing the work of God, let us not do it for personal gain but for the glory of God: "God help us in this one" (because most of the time we find ourselves doing it for our own glory) sometimes we get carried away and start doing it for personal gain, or for our own glory. Let us ask for help to preach out of good will so that He gives us the heart of a servant of the people and of the Lord, we desire to be like His Son who humbled Himself for your name's sake. Give us a heart and will to do like you showed us because you were saying these things are possible.

Christianity should Transform the World

Christians would transform the world by showing the good works they were shown by Christ the Messiah who came on earth to give an example of how the world should be lived in order for it to be a good place to live in. Sometimes people who are pagans hate their neighbours. As Christianity advanced throughout the world, cultures and civilisation improved and changed for the better, and education improved the church also improved technology, even those who do not believe in Christianity have been made to know that a person is created in the image of God. So, everyone has been made to value life of a human being. Christians built schools, churches, Hospitals and orphanages by building schools their desire was to make everyone get some form of education knowing that an educated society is a civilised society. By building hospitals, they want to improve the national health knowing that a healthy nation is a strong nation, by building orphanages they value human life knowing that a person resembles God spiritually. Christians copy all what they do from Jesus because His concern was of those who down-graded and the marginalised He wanted all the people to be at the same level, the poor to get a better life, the sick to get well, if Christians would emulate that fully they would transform the world. Christianity should be received as good news by the world because it is there to alleviate human suffering. We get out of touch with you because we start saying that it is our right yet your son never had any right. Those rights we are claiming, we are claiming them wrongly, we do not have even control of our bodies, so what rights have we got, we are just distancing ourselves from you. As believers, we have to be exemplary to none believers, not to boast, but to be able to bring them to Christ when they have seen the goodness in us, help us not to be preachers only but doers of your word. Sometimes we miss what we want because we want recognition immediately. Jesus did not want to only say these things but had to do them Himself. What He actually did, we can still dread to do it even up to this day. Let alone dying for our friends, even just helping when a friend is in need, even where I see that I am more privileged than my friend, I cannot even help, Lord, please give me the heart and the courage to help. Where am I missing my target? Lord plant your kingdom in my heart, the cross is where our sins were repaid, the devil is conquered, and Christianity is put in good shape.

The cross inaugurates the new covenant when Jesus revealed this at the last supper. He said his death would bring the new covenant. On the cross Jesus conquered sin, that is where He showed us that you can sacrifice your blood for your friend, and or your neighbour. His dying on the cross for our sins shows God's love for us, and God expects us to respond to such love by glorifying His name. That means Jesus ransomed and redeemed us, and made us to be fit for heaven or to be called the children of the highest. Jesus by doing so, made us to enter into a New Covenant with God. When Jesus dies on the cross, the new community is formed, it is called specially to public prophetic to the Christian hope of the kingdom, it is very much concerned with the alleviation of the social welfare of the community. This community started with the disciples of Jesus (Jeremiah 31:33-34) (NIV), there is a new relationship between God and His people, all our hopes were lost when He sent us His Son to redeem us. As we read the word of God, it should not be on paper only, but must be engraved in our hearts forever. This should make us know what offends our Lord and let us desist from that for that will make us unfit to be called your children. We must always strive to please him, who gave us his Holy Spirit who will give us the desire to always do good to him. We know that we had distanced ourselves from the old covenant, but your son came to renew that covenant, which if we obey it, we will be true Christians.

The cross conquers sin and death and cancels the record of debt that stood against humanity (Colossians 2:14) (NIV). Man had sinned and that sin was following us all our lives, making us subjected to slavery forever, that sin was holding us captives demanding a ransom,

Christ decided to pay the ransom and redeem us forever, His death and His resurrection was the payment of the ransom, and it is paid in full no more any demand from anybody. Sometimes we forget that we are free and allow the devil to play with our brains, and make us think that we still owe him anything. As we died with Him, it is time to rise with Him at the resurrection, otherwise the devil wants us to believe that our debt is not yet paid wanting to subject us to guilt, yet we don't owe anybody anything, we are new and clean. On the cross, Jesus bore all our sins on his body, so that we will be without sin at death. Jesus on the cross carried all our burdens and we are now set free and he conquered all spiritual forces of darkness. Understanding the cross and the resurrection as a single event is important. If at all Jesus was crucified on the cross and ended there it would not have been a full event, but now that after three days God resurrected Him from the dead, it becomes a full and complete event. (Galatians 3:13) (NIV), in those days if you were sentenced to be hanged on the cross it was a curse, so for Jesus to be hanged on the cross, He was cursed in our stead, through the death and resurrection of Christ, death is swallowed up in victory, (1 Corinthians 15:54-55) (NIV), as man had sinned, so we were condemned to death and our flesh to be corrupted in death, but by Jesus dying on the cross and resurrecting, all that has been reversed now, and we are fit for heaven.

The cross vanquishes the devil, on the cross, Christ did not only conquer sin and death, but he conquered spiritual forces of darkness. At the resurrection, Jesus defeated all the power of the devil and all forces of darkness and gave power to all who believe in Him. At Golgotha, Jesus disarmed the power of darkness, all the authorities, and put them to shame, as he triumphs over them at death. This was clearly revealed at the resurrection. (Colossians 2:14) (NIV), as man had sinned against God that made him to drift away from the Lord, but with God's love of man, He had to send His Son in order to bring him back into the fold, the covenant He had made with Adam was broken, He had to make another covenant at mount Sinai, although they had vowed to keep this one, they kept on breaking it. In the end, He had to send His Son, this time the covenant was made with His blood on the cross. As Christ rose from the dead, he is now seated at the right hand of the Father.

03

Gospel of the Kingdom

God Works in People's Lives

J esus' message was mainly that the kingdom has come, this was His central theme in the first three gospels, this is a process that God begins to work in people's lives, governs as king, then the kingdom manifests in people's lives. Sometimes we ignore that little voice that speaks to us, expecting to hear God speak to us in a loud voice. It is said to us that we should not expect someone to come from heaven to speak to us or to advise us on what course to take in our lives. Let us listen to that little voice that is the Lord speaking to us Jesus told a story of a rich man who wanted God to send someone from heaven to advise his relatives not to walk the same path as he had walked. Jesus said to him they will not listen because someone came from heaven, they must listen to those who are talking to them that is God talking to them. Let us take our conversations seriously. Jesus even said even the Son of man who had come from heaven they even killed Him, so God is speaking to us let us hear Him, and the most important thing is to listen and do what He is telling us to do. The spiritual realm where God reigns as king the fulfilment on earth of God's will, in reality, this means that God works through people that His kingdom will be seen through the good works done. This teaches us that, that's the way God wants to be known by people through the work introduced by Jesus. This Jesus' work came to the climax on the cross and at the resurrection, this has brought us closer to God. The main message of the kingdom is to repent, meaning that we have realised our wrongdoings and ask to be forgiven and promising never to repeat doing wrong things again and keep my relationship with God as close to Him as possible. If we abide by the laws of God, we are promised eternal life, if we stay pure in heart, Jesus promises to give us the authority that was given to Him from heaven and earth. This means that people will see the kingdom of heaven on you.

As the gospel is good news to us, it means that we are taken step by step and made to know how the heavenly kingdom is, slowly we are made to know that it is us who have to be transformed in order for us to qualify for the heavenly kingdom. So, when we ask for his kingdom to come, it will come because it will be us who will have transformed, but the biggest challenge we face is that we want shortcuts, we do not want to transform ourselves, but for the kingdom to come to us, while we are doing things that are contrary to what is done in heaven. The agreement is that, we were offered redemption and restoration after repentance and receiving Christ as Lord.

(John1:12 If you accept the offer from the Lord, you become a child of the highest, to be a child of God is a privilege earned by faith, yet we boast to be children of the earthly richest people. If at all we were blessed we could ask to be children of eternity by accepting Him into our hearts. With the things of God there is no compulsory of any kind, the choice is yours, to take it or leave it. When the light came it enlighten our way to salvation, John the Baptist came to bear witness to that light. He was said to be a word in the beginning, by accepting the word, you are accepting the Son of God, the Messiah, the Saviour, and the redeemer, and you are receiving the grace in its fullness, and you are receiving all the blessings from Him, like what Moses did when he came down the mountain he was shining, the same thing happens to us today we will be shining if we stay closer to Him.

If you receive Him in your heart, He will receive you into His kingdom, you will become distinct from the children of the earth, to be the son of God is a special favour. To become the son of God is a free will and of your own choice, you will inherit an in-corruptible inheritance which will be yours for ever and the Holy Spirit will be with you, to guide you for ever.

The Gospel of the Kingdom of God is with us

(John 1:8) (NIV) Although the kingdom of God is within us, it suffers the violence of the corrupt world. Why does the kingdom of God have to suffer and why should violent people make it suffer? Jesus himself is the source of eternal life, He even told people that the kingdom of heaven has come meaning that his coming means the coming of the kingdom but not all smooth as could be expected. Jesus teaches of a farmer who planted wheat, but by night an enemy planted tare, but the farmer said leave them like that it will be seen on the day of harvest. That means we have to be very careful because the devil has planted among us those who do not love the heavenly kingdom and are trying by all means to destabilise the flourishing of the gospel, but also Jesus said he is not going to do anything until the day of His coming. The reason why Jesus had come to Earth was to make us see physically what He did and for us to follow exactly as He did it. In short, the gospel means the revelation of the kingdom of God to man, since the kingdom is full of holy people, for us to qualify we have to repent in order for us to be made holy also so that we can qualify. Gospel means good news in which Jesus reveals that the kingdom has come. He revealed this to us and expects us to continue where He left off. We are struggling to continue where Jesus left off, yet we should ask for guidance because living in this corrupt world we are striving but finding ourselves on the wrong side.

Jesus is Alive, our Hope and the Truth

Jesus brought us good news like this, once you put your faith in Christ means you will understand that He brought us salvation through the gospel, the good news that He brought is that the kingdom of heaven is now within us. (John 3:16) (NIV) The reason why God sent His Son into the world is His love for the world, His love is not just an ordinary love but sacrificial love that someone gives their life for the other, God did this in order to make us prepare for eternity knowing that this life is only a beginning and is only temporal. By sending His Son into the world He wants us to be guided into eternal life, this we can only be guided if we have faith. If we had the wrong choice before, there is still time to make the right decision, to decide to follow Him in truth and in spirit and start thinking of eternity which we should be working for. Let us give ourselves to Christ and become His and His forever, that means we are preparing for eternity. The love that He has shown to us, if we would also show such love in return, that would mean meeting half way. Sometimes in life we expect to see miracles which we will never see because God works in us in ways that we may not think that it is God working among us, even when his Son came as a Messiah no one believed Him they only said He was the son of a carpenter. In life, let us value these things, go to church; read the Bible and pray provided you do this in truth and in spirit Let us know that God speaks to us with a very silent voice, but that voice is real if we obey it, we must always talk to Him, to guide us all our lives if we confess our sins, He gives us a new life which is a well transformed life and we are new creations. Most of the time we make mistakes in our lives, but God corrects us and gives us more time as He is good to us, we must be honest to Him. We must be talking to God as we walk to work as we are at work, so that means we must be talking to Him all the time of our lives so that our relationship with Him will be a closer relationship; listen to Him in music; listen to Him when others speak to us, always let us strive to be good in all our lives God works for our good in all things. Let us believe that we will be transformed, and this takes away all our worries and fears. Jesus is the king of kings and Lord of Lords who will take over all the kingdoms of this world and establish His everlasting kingdom. We need to ask for divine revelation to be on us in order to understand this because to most of us, we have to be told that the earthly governments will be taken over, as it appears to be very remote to be a reality, yet that is the truth about it. (Matthew 24:14) (NIV) Jesus expects us to do his assignment that He gave to us seriously because He said this good news has to reach everyone in all the corners of the world before He comes back. Before we expect Him to come back, we must be obedient enough to do our part so that we will not feal guilty when He asks for a report. Everyone has an assignment, Jesus commissioned His disciples and this has been passed down to us so that you and me have to give a report, what report are you giving? This message is to those believers who might say, if that is the case Christ should come now, but let them know that His thoughts are not our thoughts, although we might want that kingdom to take over now, but to Him He says this gospel of the kingdom must be preached to all nations and then shall the end come. The author is pleading with the reader that let us take up this assignment we were given by our Lord before He left. We should take this to all corners of the world before he comes back, because we will have to give a report to Him when He comes.

When Jesus said all authority is given unto him, He meant that He had the power which when seeking this power, we earthly people we would like to use this power to gain control over others and subject them to be under our feet, "God help us" Jesus meant to have power, not over but is to be the servant of the people, are we really seeking to be the servant of the people? (Mark 16:19-20) (NIV) We seem to have not reached that stage where we say I should be hungry in order for someone to eat, or for me to go to jail for someone to be free. No matter how much wealth we have, we do not want to give a penny to someone we know very well to be an orphan who has no other means to survive, we are living in a corrupt world, but we still want to be like Christ, because Christ also lived in this corrupt world, but came out pure, so we have no excuse whatsoever, we seem to want to be like Christ in words only and not in what we do yet that is where our faith hinges. Our faith should be rooted in emulating exactly liken He did, if we want to be like Him. It is the Holy Spirit we must ask to guide us all our lives. To understand it, we must try to look at it from different angles, this will make us understand it better. Jesus said, I am the way, the truth and the life, because no one comes to the Father without going through Him. We can only be saved by believing in Him as the only way to the Father.

The Gospel is Good News

(Luke 4:18) (NIV) He came with the good news that sinners can now be set free as long as they believe that there is someone who came for their sins. It is surprising that Jesus had grown in this village, but up to this date they did not recognise Him that He was the Messiah, the same thing may be happening to us to this date, that He has been with us spiritually but we cannot recognise Him, when He said this scripture is fulfilled in your eye's todays, they seemed to be very far from Him. I am praying that as this scripture has been preached to us, it is time we asked for understanding and recognise that he has come for me the poor sinner, to set me free from the bondage of Satan, and has come to rescue me from chains of the devil and set me free. (Mark 1:14-15) (NIV) It is surprising that there came John the Baptist to say that there was coming a Messiah who was very powerful that even his shoes I am not fit to loosen but still people did not understand that, still even when Jesus came, they did not even understand that, we are not being taken unawares as well because the gospel has been preached to u several times, but it appears we are still expecting someone to come from heaven so we would believe him, I pray that we be covered with the Holy Spirit so that we understand that the one that is being preached is the one we have to accept for our salvation. (Mark 1:1) (NIV) It appears we sometimes lose focus and begin to think that Jesus came for those people of long ago, as he left and went back to heave, then we seem to conclude that those are bygones now, not knowing that Jesus is alive today as He was in those days, He is alive and dwells among us today. We were dead in our sins, but there was someone who decided to leave His heavenly kingdom and decided to come and rescue us from the chains of the devil. So, the coming of Jesus Christ to the world is good news, He even said the kingdom of God has come, so His coming is good news. The four gospels were written to prove that Jesus is the Messiah the eternal king, this is strengthened with the fact of His miraculous birth, His life and teachings were beyond comparison. During His life time He performed miracles which were beyond any doubt, which were all consolidated at the cross and at his resurrection. Although the Jews expected this miraculous man to deliver them from the rule of the Romans, this did not happen as they liked, on the cross they lost all hopes, which even to this day some are still hopping for the first coming of the Messiah, yet He died on the cross to free every man from the sin's oppression.

His resurrection from the dead was a demonstration that whoever follows Him, must follow Him in truth and in Spirit, and has to have faith in Him and will also rise from the dead on the last day, and will have eternal life. Our role is to tell the people all over the world that the resurrection means salvation for every man who believes and who has faith in Him will be saved.

The four books, Matthew, Mark, Luke, and John are called the gospels, they concentrate on the teachings of Jesus Christ. A prophecy from (Daniel 2:44) (NIV). "And in the days of these kings the God of heaven will set up a kingdom which shall never be destroyed, and the kingdom shall not be left to other people; it shall break in pieces and consume all these kingdoms, and it shall stand forever". Some of the prophecies of Isaiah happened, some are happening and some are still to happen. What we are asked to do is to obey God's laws now in order to enjoy later, He is making a covenant with us, if we keep this covenant, it will mean, we are keeping good relations with our creator. In this covenant we are to turn our weapons of war into ploughshares so that we have plenty to eat, (Isaiah 2:2-4) (NIV): Even before this new covenant, God used to make covenants with His people such as when He instructed Solomon to build a temple where the ten commandments were kept in these commandments is where He would meet with His people, (2 Chronicles 5:1) (NIV). The gospels are there to tell us that the old earth will pass away and there will be a new earth where only those who are the chosen ones, will live forever, (Revelation21) (NIV).

04

Spiritual Realms

What is a Spiritual Realm?

The spiritual world, according to spiritualism, is the world or realm inhabited by spirits, both good or evil, of various spiritual manifestations. Whereas religion regards an inner life, the spirit world is regarded as an external environment for spirits. (Genesis 3) (NIV) If at all it was not for our sinful nature, we would have access to some very holy things. We must always have a desire to be surrounded by Holy things, that is, asking the Holy Spirit to guide in our walk of life. (Ephesians 6:17) (NIV) We are always fighting these unseen hidden powers which we cannot fight with tangible weapons because they are hidden forces, we must put on our spiritual amour because we are fighting with these hidden spirits. We must ask the Lord to equip us spiritually. (Revelations 12:7-9) The spiritual realms are good and evil realms; the evil spiritual realms are always attacking Christians targeting those with little faith or the weaker ones. Christians must realise that even though the devil is trying, he was defeated at the resurrection, that is the reason why he is targeting the weaker. (Genesis 1:27) (NIV) To say that God created man in His own image does not mean a physical image, but to be like Him in spirit, because God is spirit, so, when we want to communicate with Him, we have to do that in spirit and in truth. Because man was made in the image of God, he was given dominion over every creation on earth. So, a man must always consult God when he wants to make informed decisions so that they must be guided decisions. A realm is a kingdom, usually things that are more of the spirit.

Spirituality is a broad concept of a belief in something beyond the self. It may involve religious traditions cantering on the belief in higher power, but it can also involve holistic belief in an individual connection to others and to the world as a whole. Your spiritual eyes provide wisdom and insight, as well as deepen your spiritual connecting.

Examples of spirituality include:

- asking deep questions about topics such as suffering; and what happens after death? After death, the soul leaves the physical body and is taken to a place where it awaits the judgement day. When close to your death you might see things that others do not see.
- Depending on what relationship you had with your loved ones who have gone, you will have deepening connection with them when close to your death.

It is not advisable that when someone is grieving, you have to be of more listening to them, until such time. Do not say so many things at once for you might say something that might hurt them and it will lose its meaning of trying to show that you are experiencing compassion and empathy for them.

Some twenty-four hours before death you might see visions which can only be seen by a person who is dying, figures are apparently seen which have the express purpose of collecting the dying person taking them on a journey through physical death. Sometimes they see things which people who are not dying cannot see, they might see you smiling at something they cannot see, that mean those dying will be experiencing and feelings of interconnectedness and feelings of owe and wonder.

What is Spirituality?

Spirituality involves the reception of a feeling that there is something greater than myself or believing that I am inferior to something. Something more to being human than sensory experience and that the greater whole of which we are part is cosmic or divine in nature. An opening of the heart is an essential aspect of true spirituality. Through the atonement we can become like our heavenly Father if we keep our part of the covenant. To become more like Him means to take on His nature-the divine nature. Associated with the divine nature are some spiritual attributes, which we can pray to obtain and strive to possess. A being of supernatural powers or attributes believed in and worshipped by people especially a male deity thought to control some part of nature or reality. By virtue of being created in the image of God that means we already have some divine this attribute could either be male or female Sometimes we under rate ourselves, by this we mean that you must put yourself where you are supposed to be, this does not necessarily mean that you boast but to humble yourself. (2 Peter 1:4) (NIV) The devil desires to corrupt us so he keeps on telling us lies that we cannot be of a divine nature yet or Lord want us to be divine. Whenever we are pursuing this divine nature, we have to bear in mind that we are living in a corrupt world which wants us to be against our Lord. We have to bear in mind that the new covenant wants us to be like our divine Father if we keep our part of the covenant.

If you feal connected to something larger than yourself, you are driven by the highest level of achievement greater than the people around you, whether that means God, spirituality, or a set of values you live by. Sometimes people are working towards some larger goal that is more important one individual person. When you want to create something bigger than yourself you have to: open your heart to self-discovery; create a purpose statement; follow your passion or make a real commitment. Different people have different beliefs such as: Believing in God, believing in magic; believing in miracles; believing in art; believing in humanity. Human beings are also part of the universe. People who have meaning and purpose in their lives are happier and feel more in control and get more out of what they do, they also feel less stress and anxiety and depression. Trying to find the meaning and purpose of life is about being part of something you believe in that is bigger than yourself. It is discovered that people who have meaning and purpose in life are happier, get more out of what they do and feel more in control. This sometimes gives you a complete life, or contribute to actual human being with an extra ordinary personality or some other distinguishing features that sets them apart from others. To be described as such could give you a lofty tribute in life. If someone is larger than life that attracts a lot of attention because they are more exciting or interesting than most people.

Spirituality means we are always seeking something bigger than us; it also means that we always seek connection with them. This might give us positive information this gives us some sort of wisdom and peace, most of the who take part, or as part of spirituality are larger than life. When it is like that, you are always searching for the meaning of life. A spiritual experience is being connected with God or dedicated to a religious purpose and so deserving great respect or reverence, (sacred), or beyond or above the range of normal or physical human experience or higher than normal (transcendent) or without making it difficult, a deep sense of aliveness and a state of being connected with each other having internal connections.

It often appears that spiritual life is (intricately) linked to our association with the church, temple, mosque or synagogue. Develop it fully in prayer and you will find comfort in a personal relationship with God. Seek for a sense of (purpose). Try to dive deep into it and you will find that you improve your relationship with God.

Most characters in his movies are larger than life: These heavenly characters are inspired that is why they are more than life itself.

How to find meaning in life: There are so many things in life which want to make you unhappy, but if you bow to them, you will stay an unhappy person. On earth, things are not perfect, so if you want to wait until they are perfect, you will never be happy, make yourself happy against all the adds. Things being unequal, you must choose to be happy, you will have to stay calm and deal with things that need your attention. Practise happiness and stay with things under your control, there are stories that you cannot overcome sadness, when you can. Sometimes in life you have some gifts and some talents which you have not explored yet. Choose the people to associate with who can make your life happy, spend time with them. From what they do to you can easily tell that these people cannot add any meaning to my life. Plan your life and not to wait for someone to plan it for you. Be good to others and give them a help from deep down your heart Helping others is good because you will make progress in life. Do your own life assessment, this will help you find your own direction in your own life.

1. Learn the lesson on happiness: Happiness is a skill you can learn, practise and get better at. It is always good for you to look on the brighter side of things that will help you to stay cheerful and avoid stress and depression.

2. Follow your gifts and talents: Every person has been given a gift by God, but only that we tend to think that others are more gifted than us, yet God wants every talent to help the world grow. Let us use our gifts fully for the good of doing God's will. God wants us to use our gifts and talents for the benefit of others. Strive to put that into practice.

3. Make great connections: The principle of striving to make great connection will help you build connections that last and will have a positive impact on your life.

4. Goal setting: When you make your goals make them achievable and attainable.

5. Help others: Helping others is not only good for them and good for things to do, it also makes us happier and healthier too. Helping others helps to build strong communication. That will make a happier and a good society for every one you can share ideas.

6. Do something different. Make sure you are not in toxic relationships you might think that if you are in a toxic relationship, you might be able to change it, but in most cases, you will end up being diluted yourself, so to avoid this, you better keep away from such relationships. Do not put things away until tomorrow, tomorrow has its own things, feel in charge of your day, by feeling you will get more things done. Do not feel that I cannot do this or I am not good enough brush that way of thinking from you. Do not think negative thoughts about your body or about your ability. Brush aside all thoughts that are negative about you.

7. Quit watching TV. Make yourself a time table to watch Tv, make yourself a timer and stick to that so that you give yourself time for other things in life try to be more social. To give yourself a limited time on TV is to try to give time for other things in life. Some people have an average time of 5 hours a day on TV, that is a lot in a day. Change that habit and change your life for the better.

8. Do something you have always wanted to do, we must always strive that we must accomplish something that we always want to do, sometimes we keep on saying, I will do it, I will do it but time runs out. There are things you have always wanted to do in life, if you reflect on them, have you achieved them? Something always comes up that you never wanted to do, ask yourself, is it worth it? Ask yourself if you have put more effort in it? if not put more effort, do not give up, keep on trying, one day you will succeed

Do you ever wonder on earth why you are here; you know like how to find meaning in life, or your purpose in life? Or why so you actually exist on this planet.

These are probably the most subtle, and yet profound questions people ask themselves every day and I can bet you, there is probably many different answers to these questions as there are people asking them too. Let us make your experience the answer.

How the Spirit Develops in People

Prayer is a way of talking to God, knowing that He is person we become satisfied that we are talking to someone, it becomes something different when you lack that vision that you are with someone. If we know that He is Spirit, we have to adjust ourselves to be spiritual. We have to create positivity in our lives, trying to shape our future spiritually and positively this will help our emotions and immoralities. In your mind create something that is unique to yourself and you alone, awaken your own spiritual things.

That will enable us to communicate at the same level. There are some things that a praying person has to bear in mind, is that although He hears you now, but He sets His own time, knowing that He is the one who sets times, since everything has its own time, the problem arises when we try to set times for Him, and how He has to answer our prayers, we want our prayers answered the way we want them answered. Our prayers might not be answered the way we asked them to be, it is because He knows us better and knows what is better for us. Sometimes we want our prayers answered so we can be exactly as our neighbour, which is not the way He does His thing. What we have to realise is that if He opens other avenues for us, we have to pursue that and see what He has in store for us. The best way to communicate with Him is to know Him, and to know who He is, to know the way He answers and the time He answers and the way He answers, then that means you have grown spiritually. Spend time with Him so you will get to know Him better, the godly things are like our life application, you spend time with people you will get to know them better. The same applies to God, you spend a lot of time with Him, you will get to know Him better the same applies to spiritual things, the more your spiritual things the more you grow spiritually.

The human spirit includes, the way we reason and understand things, our mental powers, strong feelings such as joy, anger, sadness as distinguished from reasoning or knowledge, unpleasant emotions caused by threat of danger, an intense enthusiasm for something and imaginations or ideas to bring up something, this is considered to be the mental functions of awareness, insight, understanding, judgement and other reasoning powers.

Also, the growth of the spirit depends on how you value things, how do you value God and all the Godly things? The way you value things will mean that you yourself will be making the spirit grow, valuing things could be both physically and mentally.

(2 Peter 3:1- 18) (NIV) The fact that God does not answer prayers the way we expect, might make the spirit of some fail to grow because of thinking that He is not there when in actual fat He is spirit. The advice is not giving God a time table, infect we have to fit into His own time. To grow in spirit is also to stay alert knowing that there will be a second coming, this is part of growing in spirit.

In most cases spiritual growth is done by you depending how you take things what you want to achieve, set your goals set up your mind to make it grow what goals you have set satisfy yourself that you have achieved it, do not under rate know that you the child of God and knowing that He loves you. We have to trust in the Lord knowing that His grace is sufficient, to have faith in Him is to grow in spirit as well. No matter how we try to grow our spirit, we have to remember that we are living in a corrupt world which tries always to pull us down, so we have to resist that temptation.

I believe there is another realm of reality that we see only dimly. It is a spiritual reality. To know that there a creator or ruler of the universe, this maker of the universe must be revered and all the glory go to Him now and for ever. Much is unexplainable in our physical world. Science when it is honest must say something things cannot be proven or disproven. The spiritual realm operates by different laws.

The Earthly Kingdom is Geographically Bound

It does not necessarily mean that they work together, but that they contrast between them, meaning that they work in totally different ways. (John 18:33-37) (NIV) Sometimes the earthly people take the wrong view of the heavenly kingdom, because of not knowing how the heavenly kingdom works they tend to mix the political kingdom with the heavenly kingdom this in the end makes a great contrast of the two kingdoms, which will require divine intervention to be able to understand the two. What led Jesus to be crucified was just a misunderstanding because when Jesus said His kingdom was not of this world, they would have released and would have understood him straightaway, because if His kingdom was not of this world, they would have released and known Him because that means He was not going to take their earthly kingdom. That means they unknowingly killed Him, what were they expecting to gain after they had killed Him? If they had a revelation, they would have asked Him to accommodate them in to His kingdom, but no one could, then that was a lost opportunity. Are we not losing the same opportunity by not asking Jesus for the right thing? The man on the cross asked the right question, He asked to be remembered by Jesus in his kingdom, because he asked a direct question he was answered directly, that on the same day he would be with Jesus in paradise. Sometimes, because we suffer some pains in this corrupt world, we tend to ask Jesus to take us from the pain of this corrupt world, not asking Him to promise us the eternity of our souls. If we have a promise for the eternity of our souls, we would have asked for the right thing. The kingdom of heaven prefers to work spiritually with some gentleness. Here they are mentioned together in order for the reader to see the contrast that is there between the two kingdoms. There is a big contrast that one wonders if they will ever work together, to achieve their goals, the earthly kingdom will make sure it will work over, not under in order to accomplish its goal.

The Heavenly Kingdom is Spiritually Bound

God rule for ever, which means, the rule of God lasts eternity it is sovereign it rules all the universe. God is the undeniable monarch of all creation (Romans 13:1) His kingdom will last forever, everything we see was created by Him. We have to acknowledge His rule and accept Him in our hearts so as for Him to dwell in us (John 18:36) (NIV) Since we have never heard of any boundaries in heaven so from the answer of Jesus to Pilate it is clear that it has no boundaries like the kingdoms of this world. Sometimes on earth we fight for boundaries so if there are no boundaries in heaven that means there is no need for fighting at all. It is interesting to note that this kingdom is in the believers' hearts which answers the question whether it has physical boundaries If the heavenly kingdom is in our hearts, what we must do must always reflect that the kingdom is in our hearts. We must always ask ourselves, what I am doing, does it show to people the kingdom of heaven, if not then I have to change. (Matthew 4:17) (NIV) Where the heavenly kingdom works under and applies take it or leave, the earthly kingdom applies the take it, way of doing things without a choice.

Physical boundaries such as mountain ranges and lakes, national and subnational political boundaries that establish local autonomy may prevent the violation of cultural norms that cause friction between groups and promote self-determination, inhibiting the triggers of violence. This description of physical boundaries shows clearly the contrast that is there between the earthly kingdom and the heavenly kingdom. Unlike the earthly kingdom, the heavenly kingdom is invisible but alive because its works are visible when it is working in us, our works will tell that we are filled with the heavenly kingdom.

05

The Rich Man and Lazarus

Wealth is like any other thing you might think of, wealth itself is not bad but the way you handle it is what matters. It should not change your way of thinking, it is there to make us to live a life, and not to forget that those who do not have wealth also wanted to have it but failed. For you to have it was not your cleverness but only coincidence. May we be reminded that when we came into the world, we found riches were there, and we must be reminded that when we go, we do not take anything with us but to leave everything here, so why boasting and forgetting that these things are not ours, we are only temporal stewards of them before we return to where we came from. It is better to ask ourselves if we brought anything, if not, then where is the boasting coming from, with things that do not belong to us this must teach us a very valuable lesson which would help our souls. When Jesus said, it is easier for a camel to enter through the eye of a needle than for a rich man to enter heaven, He meant that we have to be cautious with riches that they should not lead us astray. Riches are not bed, but it is the way we use them that may defile us. "Lazarus means God has helped us" Martha and Mary rejoiced because of what God had done to them.

It is of no relevance to look down upon others because to be rich or to be poor, all is beyond our control, because it is unto the Lord to either make us poor or rich. It is unto Him to raise the poor from the dust to the very highest level or to make the richest poor, we have no control of a single thing. When He gives us wealth, He wants us to share with those who do not have, so He is putting the responsibility on us to do His will, are we not becoming greedy and forgetting our responsibility, let us be reminded.

The rich man learnt a very valuable lesson, but it was too late, he forgot to be humble instead he became arrogant because he was carried away by selfishness. We lose nothing if we are humble and generous to others, it is always good to ask to be guided on how to use the wealth that we have accumulated otherwise it is going to be a rope to hang ourselves, yet we all want wealth to help us.

What is the Meaning of the Kingdom of God is Within You?

This tells us that if that is the case then we have to be very cautious and know that, this has to be manifested to people from us. This has got two meanings, which are: Jesus was representing the kingdom of heaven and He was already amongst them, with them not even noticing that this was the Messiah well promised thousands of years earlier. As He had been with them for some time, they should have been familiar with the authority that he had shown that He was representing the kingdom of heaven. Jesus tells us that when we repent and believe, the kingdom of God is within us. Let God reign in your heart then the kingdom God has come. For this kingdom to happen, examine yourself, where you find you have gone wrong you must repent, because that is the only way you can have relationship with Him.

Also, when He said the kingdom of God is within you, He meant that since he had taught everything about heaven, it was expected to have already been taken into the hearts of the people that there would be purity in their hearts that whatever they would be doing or saying would manifest the kingdom of heaven. In other words, He was saying we are ambassadors of the heavenly kingdom, the heavenly kingdom must be seen in our deeds and words. They misunderstood Jesus because they had their own expectation, of a political leader. That is the reason why the author is pleading with the reader not to have preconceived conclusions other than going with what is there. Clearly, as Christians we are expected to represent the kingdom so that people see the kingdom coming from our hearts, people should see the kingdom from us in such a way that they will say the kingdom of heaven has come. We have to let people know that someone has already paid for those sins, so it's time for us to receive that with clean hearts.

(Hebrews 9:28) This verse requires us to put our trust in Jesus for us to get salvation and eternal life, because that is our goal. Jesus came for the purpose of showing us the heavenly kingdom or showing us the way to the heavenly kingdom (John 18:36). When Christians are being persecuted, we as Christians we must suffer with them because all Christians are all brothers in Christ, like parts of our body, when one part of the body has been injured, the whole body will suffer. The whole body will accompany that part to the hospital, when that part is healed, the whole body will rejoice. We are asking the Lord to hear our prayers for the whole body of Christianity to be under His control, (Matthew 24:5-14). We know that without His control, we can be swayed about by false prophets, Jesus knew that what happened in the Old Testament that there were false prophets, is still happening today. These days they are more tactful than those of the Old Testament, because of the technology that has developed.

Beware of False Prophets

These false prophets are increasing and they are more tactful that you may think that they are genuine prophets yet it is only love of money. According to what Jesus said, it is not these false prophets, but it is our ears which are itching to hear these things. It is because we are looking for quick solutions to our problems, yet if we are following His footsteps, Jesus never looked for quick solutions, but to do His Father's will. (2 timothy 4:3-4) we tend to turn our ears from the truth, there are so many winds of doctrine which are tossing us around, we have to earnestly ask for guidance so that we follow the right direction, and to follow the truth of the word, there is nowhere we can do it alone without the guidance of the Lord, to faith fully and honestly ask for His guidance. Without the guidance we will end up receiving the wrong doctrines where we will end up being confused. (Ephesians 4:11-14) (NIV) they claim to have revelation from the Lord yet they are misleading and will deceive many, by their fruits you shall see them, these church members, are they really following the scriptures as they are? Those scriptures were inspired to help us not to be swayed all over, when they want to accumulate earthly wealth. (Matthew 24:5-14) (NIV) What we are seeing today is that, so many prophets who have arisen is not something new, Jesus said, when you see these things happen do not be moved or follow them. False prophets were there in the Old Testament. There were prophets of Baal who had a very big following and yet they were false, our days are not an exception, when people are oppressed, they tend to follow anything that comes promising them liberty, but will deceive many.

Sometimes these hard times come because of the wrath of God, we have to come to Him and repent, sometimes it is a collective sin to the Lord, but if one man may be filled with the Holy Spirit, he may intercede for the whole nation may be saved. Lord fill one man with your Holy Spirit so that he may intercede for your people.

(Jeremiah 23:16) (NIV) People were fooled and deceived were

given vain promises, people were filled with vain hopes of peace which did not come to pass. People were given promises of good times ahead which did not come from the Lord, and drew many away from the truth.

All the Glory Must be to God

What Jesus did, to die for other people's sins and the way He died was so painful and so shameful, that He deserves all the glory. God created us for His glory, but instead, man chose to rely on himself and by seeking his own glory. People very much want to make a name for himself, but He sent His Son to show us the way and to let us know that God said, let us make man in our own image in order for the man to represent God on earth. It is misguided to try to seek glory for ourselves yet we have already been glorified by representing the heavenly kingdom on earth, instead what we have to do is to act responsibly. When man was given dominion, he was expected to respond by behaving responsibly, there is no point in seeking another glory while we have been given the glory already. We have to know what the goals of God are, if we do then if we act accordingly, then we will be in good relationship with our Lord who loved us before we did. If we are doing things against His will, then our eternity is in question, yet all what we are striving for is eternity, if we lose that, it means we have lost what we were sacrificing for all our lives. Let us know the ultimate goal of our creation what we were created for, what happens in life is that we get shifted from our original without knowing that we have shifted thinking that we are still there. I must always strive to bring my heart and my behaviour into alignment with the will of God, according to what He created me for. It is better to reflect and see what you went through in your life and see that the grace of God was upon you. You will know that it is time to give all the glory to Him, He has gone through trying times for you, and you forget that and seem to have survived with your cleverness.

Jesus Left it to us to Decide our Destiny

(John 3:16) (NIV), tells us that we can only get eternal life by believing in such love and by emulating such love that means we are following in His footsteps of loving unconditionally. True love never says, I love you because you love me too, but without getting any return from the one you love you still love that subject. To be at par with Jesus we have to make sure the needy are looked after, the widows, the orphans, the prisoners, because Jesus said, He came for the oppressed He has come to set slaves free, His coming is the year of jubilee to them, by the coming of the kingdom they are set free.

(Matthew 7:15-20) (NIV) We should evaluate false teachers by examining their lives. Jesus left it to us to decide, and to be watchful, are they modelling their lives to what they teach, it is difficult to pick them up but we have to persevere we will still know them by their fruits. Jesus gave us a very good example, for a bad tree will never produce good fruits. Neither a good tree to bring forth bad fruit, these days many people are quoting the Bible, but it is for us to ask God to give us the revelation so that we understand of their interpretation of the scriptures. When we have the revelation, it will be easier to detect false prophet because it will be you who will have the revelation in order to find the true interpretation from those prophets. These days many people are very eager to quote the Bible when-ever they want to build a name for themselves or to make glory for themselves not the glory of the Lord. That is why the author pleads with the reader to always ask for divine intervention, because without the aid of the Holy Spirit you cannot be able to tell the true prophet or false prophet. These people are putting on sheep's clothing, yet inside they are ravening wolves, we must not lose focus that we are working for eternity. These false prophets would like to take our eternity away from us with us not knowing, until that day of judgement when everything will be made clear. They study the situation, what the people want to hear is what they tell people and say it is a prophecy and people easily believe them. They were there during Jesus' time, they are still there today, let us be vigilant so that our eternity is not stolen away from us. Most of these false prophets are motivated by want of money than the eternity of the people, you will see them by what they are. What they are seeking is the glory for themselves, not the glory for the Lord who died for our cause.

What the Kingdom of Heaven Means in Matthew 13

When taken loosely, Mark and Luke refer to the kingdom of God when Matthew refers to the same thing, but calls it the kingdom of heaven, so these three refer to the same thing differently. That is why it is referred to as loosely the same, that means you can say either without altering the meaning of the story. This might have a slight change when we start going into analysis. In Christianity it means the spiritual realm where God reigns as sovereign as king or the fulfilment on earth of God's will. The kingdoms of glory: the (celestial) kingdom of the highest, the (terrestrial) the middle of the kingdoms. (Matthew 7:21-23) (NIV) Let us make sure our relationship with Jesus is a true relationship that will last until the judgement day. Jesus is interested in what we do than what we say, we should have a personal relationship with Him. On the day of judgement, it is only our relationship with Him that will save us, we have to accept that He is the saviour If we accept that He is the saviour, that means that we accept all His commandments, keep them and do them. Faith in Him is what counts on the judgement day. Characteristics and values of the kingdom will be:

- faith, complete trust and confidence in Him, the spirit must convict us to know that He is our saviour
- simplicity of a child, purity, Jesus even said, to enter the kingdom we have to be like children, which means children are pure in the eyes of God. Everything the children do they do it innocently, without having a heavy heart towards others.

- belongs to those who suffer: who are like the children because Jesus said let the children come to me for the kingdom of heaven is of such.
- love God and love your neighbour: Love God with all your heart and with all your soul, love your neighbour as yourself.
- honest and truth refrain from all lies whatever you say, is how it is or how it should be
- humility: Meaning that in Christianity we must humble ourselves humbling yourself to what God says to you, this will lead to riches, honour and long life.
- joy in others' achievements: It is a sign of good breeding to have joy when others have achieved, tomorrow it will be your achievement and they will rejoice on you.
- wealth and ambition must be sacrificed, to love worldly things that you forget that they stay while your soul goes, ensure that those things will not lead you stray.

The kingdom of heaven can be entered through repentance and by living what we preach obeying everything as taught in the scriptures. It is up to us today to be convicted that he is in us and us in Him then we have built a good relationship. Jesus likened the heavenly kingdom with the things we do in our everyday lives, so that we can be able to grasp the meaning. There are times that when the word is preached to us it will not even enter into our hearts, that means it is likened unto the seed that fell on dry ground, were not covered with any soil, and were picked by the birds straight away, sometimes the devil takes our word even before it gets into us. Some that fell on rocky ground germinated, but their roots were not deep enough, when the sun came, they dried up and died. Sometimes we hear the word but without holding on to it firmly, the devil will have it as easy target to take the word away from us.

06

Kingdom Rules

The Kingdom of the World Seeks to Control Behaviour

That means the subjects of this world are playing into the hands of their controller who is the devil, who love to make things of this so attractive so as to lure us into doing things that do not please the Lord. The behaviours result from natural motivations and internal conviction; no law can accomplish that. It is a common view that communism is man's attempt to re-establish the kingdom of heaven on earth as given to the first man… (Luke 22:28-30) (NIV). How the worldly leadership is groomed will make it different from the heavenly leadership. The leaders of the world are selfish, often arrogant when clawing their way to the top. The current world leaders are talking of cutting the world violence in half by 2030, if this does not end on paper, and it could become a reality, then we are going to say our prayers are answered. We always pray that your kingdom come, that would mean that the heavenly kingdom will be ruling on earth because according to the scriptures, violence is an example of an earthly kingdom. We are praying day and night for God to bridge the gap that exists between the heavenly kingdom and the earthly kingdom. If we could have selfless leaders, who have the welfare of their fellow mates at heart, the world was going to be a place full of happiness worth living in. World leaders, if someone has an idea, they want to turn it into theirs and get all the praises as if they were the ones who had that idea originally, so the credit goes to them. Although slavery was abolished, it was only abolished on paper, but in people's inner feelings it still exists. The slave masters wanted to get rich on the strength of the slave, this is still happening, the rich would like to maximise their profit on the labour of the poor giving the peanut sort of a wage, portraying that they are not slaves, yet in reality they are slaves.

Leadership has to do it by examples; hence, it will be easy to manage because they will be following your example, and managing people will not be difficult. If a leader tries to be humble, people tend to take advantage because they are also corrupted with the world and start misbehaving, for the world to be a happy place to live in, it should come from both sides. When a leader becomes humble, as a reciprocal people have to respond by responding positively, if these two are combined, the world was going to be a happy place to live in, like as it is in heaven. The personality traits of good leaders should be sincere, modesty, fairness, a leader should really seek to be truthful, and this should come from the bottom of their hearts not pretending, they should combine honesty and good humility. Contrary to Christianity the leadership is the one who services the best. Styles of leadership differ greatly, that is, leading through public speaking or through administering, some through relationships. All Christian leaders need a servant's heart, this should involve asking the people how you would serve them better in the future. When dealing with other people always ask for a servant's heart, a servant is always willing to serve than a leader too willing to serve, so when looking for church leaders, we should look for those with a servant's heart. Where ever we are let us be willing to serve, it will make a difference in the future. Think of being helpful in all circumstances, this makes a difference in our lives. If we are modelling our lives on Jesus, He was a servant of the people, His mission here on earth was to serve, what is your mission? If we are following Jesus' footsteps, that is what we should model our lives on that rock. Most worldly leaders suffer under the control of Satan, making people to lust after all the worldly riches so that they boast of what they have and did and what they have accomplished in life. Always Satan makes his things appear like they are very good, in the beginning, because he does not want to show the bad side of his action at the beginning, or neither does he show the end of the film, that it ends in a tragedy. You need to follow Jesus in such a way that you become a family member of the heavenly kingdom. (Ephesians 2:1-5) (NIV) We require regeneration in our lives in order to qualify for the kingdom of heaven. Also, in (John chapter 3:3) (NIV), Nicodemus was told by Jesus to be born again, which means there has to be a regeneration, there has to be a transformation in your life. Transformation means if you look back, you will notice or reflect on what you did wrong and repent, repentance means you want to have a good relationship with God, if God accepts, it will mean you are being accepted into the heavenly family. If you are deeply involved in Christianity, you will be transformed in your character in such a way that your character and behaviour are like that of the heavenly family. The heavenly Father wants us to be pure because He wants us to be ambassadors of His kingdom on earth. Let us live on this earth in such a way that we are foreigners, representing our heavenly country as ambassadors, ambassadors know their country better in order to represent their country. Are we representing the heavenly kingdom here on earth?

Ambassadors of the heavenly kingdom on earth

The example of an ambassador is a clear example because whenever one represents a country, they must be the people who know their country well, and must have love for their country, so that they will be representing what they know better and what they love. Jesus said this in plain language, because He knew that people would very much need to believe on miraculous things. Jesus said those people you are with everyday are the people who are ambassadors of the heavenly kingdom. He says the message they bring to you is the message of eternal life, it only depends on how you accept the message, not who brings it. He wants us to have faith, because without faith nothing happens until you yourself have faith. Normally when ambassadors in a foreign country, they represent their country, that means they cannot represent their country if they do not know their country well. For us to represent the heavenly kingdom we must know it well, and we must be able to tell that there is every happiness in that country. The difference with those people with the people of this world is that they praise God Day and night, they love one another because they copy it from Jesus who came to give us an example, He loves the poor, the oppressed. Galatians 5:22-23) (NIV) we are being taught to represent the heavenly kingdom. The angels do a lovely Job because they are sent to do the work of the heavenly kingdom, so we must also be able to be working for the heavenly kingdom wherever we are and whatever we do is not for us but for the Lord and for the heavenly kingdom. Those different gifts we have, we must use them to serve others because that is the reason why we were given those different gifts in order for the heavenly work to be done on earth. We are faithful stewards of God's grace in its various forms.

What is God's Personal Reign on Earth?

When we talk of God's personal reign on earth, we mean that He will be fulfilling His covenants that He made with the people. If people here on earth do the will of God and do His work whole heartedly then it is God's personal reign on earth. Infect, people are doing this in response to what God did to us or is doing to us because of His love to us, because when He had seen that we were under the bondage of Satan, He gave His Son ransom us and redeem us, so whatever we might be doing is to reciprocate the love that was shown that was given to us. By God's love on earth there is peace and love He rules with justice and peace, His rule is fully accomplished on earth, God wants to spend time with you, so allow Him to be with you on one to one so you can always say what you want, always say Lord speak your servant hears. What God does to us is good for us or for you and me. After being with Him and listening to Him let His kingdom rule in you, if He does that, then His kingdom has come on earth, so there will be no more saying your kingdom come because the kingdom will have come already. God will always use people here on earth to get His work done, we must be able to say I am here Lord send me, and we honestly say it, then the Lord is happy to use us as He wishes, sometimes we get carried away and start expecting a reward, let us ask for the devil not to infiltrate our minds so that we carry on the will of God. In Christianity the spiritual realm over which God reigns as king is the fulfilment of God's will on earth. If God reigns on earth, there will be peace because His rule is just and loving. For the kingdom of God to rule on earth, is a divine gift not a human achievement. God has to rule over our hearts first, then what we will be doing will be the product of that rule in our hearts, that means there should be a development of a new social order which is based on unconditional love. If we respect each other, treating each other with brotherly love and accepting that God is ruling in my heart then the heavenly kingdom is on earth. Ours has to be a society of abundance, sharing, loving, gentleness, peace-making, and joy, there has to be equality rather than domination. This is what we may call the values of the kingdom, they differ greatly from the values of the earthly or worldly empires or kingdoms. For the kingdom of God to reign on earth, it is us who must always strive to lead by examples by living a righteous life all the time by living a positively happy life. (John 1:8) (NIV) John the baptizer was not himself the light but leading to the light. As we are, we are leading unbelievers to the light, this light is Jesu Christ. (Joshua 1:8) (NIV) When Joshua was being given instructions by God on his taking over from Moses, he was told that he must be acquainted with the scripture so that he knows what God want If God is reigning in us spiritually, all our deeds will be guided by the Holy Spirit. For Him to be in our hearts is for us to allow Him to reign in us is where the secret lies, accept Him in your heart first. Spend time with Him in talking to Him in prayer and to reading His Word in the Bible, be humble, be kind to others love others. These things can easily be forgotten, so it's up to you to keep on reminding yourself. It is only in you where you can see the reign of God.

The Earthly Kingdom imitates the Heavenly Kingdom

When we want to represent the heaven on earth, we must do exactly what is done by the heavenly beings. Everyone's name who was ever born and ever will be born is written in the book of life. So, every individual starts out with their names already written in the Book of Life. However, it can be removed (blotted out) from the Book of Life. It is clear that whoever is saved, will have their name remain in the Book of Life." When you obey God's commands and watch your life confess your sin, and live right the holy spirit will lead you and your name will be written in the Book of Life. The reason why the people of this earth would like to do what is done in heaven is because the heavenly kingdom operates within the spiritual realms. If things are operated within the spiritual realm means that they are operating within the confines of those whose things are operated by the Holy Spirit. As we always ask for the kingdom of the Holy one to come that means our prayers would have been answered. We expect God to manifest Himself through the deeds of man on earth because that was all about Jesus' teaching that the kingdom of God is already within us, only that we ask for His works to be seen showing that He is within us.

We are surrendering ourselves to God so that His will must be the one that has to be done not as we wish to be done but His will. When we ask, your kingdom come we expect it to come immediately, yet the Lord makes His plans well ahead of all our expectations. When we see, that things have not happened to our expectations, we start to despair and start saying the Lord has not answered our prayers, (Luke 3:15) (NIV). The gospel that must be preached on earth is that the kingdom of heaven has come. This means that it is in us so it must manifest to the people because of our deeds. We pray that it would be opened to us Spiritually so that we will know that His kingdom is not to be likened unto the kingdoms of this earth. Regardless of the fact that Jesus was with them for three years, they never understood His mission. His mission was to establish the heavenly kingdom on earth, yet their expectations were that He should rule Israel politically. When that did not happen, and he was led to the cross to Calvary, and was crucified, they were very disappointed, this was revealed on the way to Emmaus. The conversation which Jesus joined was that of disappointment that they never expected Him to be led like a sheep to the slaughter without offering any resistance, this was not to their expectations. Jesus tried to explain to them that for ruling Israel politically was not His mission on earth, but to rule over our souls, and win them for eternal life. The author is pleading with the reader to ask for a revelation so that we know exactly what we mean when we say your kingdom come, we are asking the Lord to transform us so that we know that the kingdom is not asking for something we do not know. (Revelation 21:27) (NIV) We must strive to have our names written in the book of life; how can we have our names in the book of life? (Revelation 13:8) (NIV), without any provocation, we just create enemies for ourselves, as we ask for the kingdom to come, we must make it come ourselves. This comes from the way we treat others, because that is the way we want to be treated. The problem with the kingdom of the world is that it creates enemies for itself, then starts crying foul when those enemies they have created are at them. Some of the battles that are being fought by the earthly kingdom could be avoided, start treating everyone like a friend, do not pretend to be friendly, but really friendship. A bigger percentage of the results of such behaviour are positive, but the positivity of such results has been initiated by you, because it is you who initiated it in the first place, the other side will only be unhappy with no hope of succeeding (despondence) to your action. The good thing in staying in harmony with others is that even the heavenly beings will stay in harmony with you. Obey Gd's will, do God's will and He will very like to make you, His child. As Jesus said, me and my Father will come and stay in you, that will mean you are in them, that is good news.

We very much try to avoid being bankrupt financially, yet care not about being bankrupt in spirit, yet that affects our eternal life. We have to examine ourselves how bankrupt are we spiritually. Some of the things we do sometimes display how much we are spiritually bankrupt. It is good to always strive to do good things all the time, because what you make will make you, yet it is you who made it in the first place. We are expected to respect one another, if we always try to create that environment, it will build you, instead of building others. Always choose who to walk with, because if you walk in the company of those who are wise, you will also be wise, leave those who cannot give you wisdom, so that you do not suffer harm. (Proverbs 22:24-25) (NIV) To be good must not be a fear of punishment, but must be a desire for the glory of the highest.

The Earthly Subjects are Striving to Stay as Pure as the heavenly subjects

We all know that the heavenly people stay as pure as they can, we would like to emulate that, but the devil will always want to implant some doubts, making us think that it is impossible to stay as pure as the heavenly people, so the devil plays with our brains because he knows that if he has captured our way of thinking then he has won us over, yet those are the devil's lies, we are still the children of God. We believers we should always be focusing on what matters for our souls, let us set our minds on the kingdom always and not to be distracted from focusing on the heavenly things that matter to our lives. In life what you practise in is what you get and is what you become experienced in, so if you are practising Godly things your deeds will always be Godly. (Colossians 3:1-4) (NIV) the devil plays with our brains so that we keep on thinking that we cannot do any holy things, so we subjected to believing that we the children of sin we cannot do anything fruitful. Let us believe that Christ came to set up His rule on earth, we can be like Him if we follow His ways of doing things. There is no way He can turn and say He does not know us, yet He is the one who taught us that if we confess our sins, He is faithful enough to make us clean. What He wants is for us to confess our sin, not to say He knows my sins, but we must confess them, that means we have shown some remorse. Let us bring the presence of God in our lives by trying to stay pure so as to stay near Him all the time. By asking Christ to stay in us means we are saying that He rose from the dead and now living with the Father, we should also rise with Him and that we should also be living with the Father. That is to be true followers of Christ who will follow Him in every step. Christ wants us to be as pure as He is, so He transforms our bodies so that we will qualify to be heavenly beings. To try to follow the example of the saviour is to strive for perfection, knowing that when we are perfect, we are fit for eternal life. We must keep on trying to be as perfect as our God is perfect because He wants us to be like Him if we do that will mean that we will have overcome the temptations of this world meaning that we will have outwitted the devil and all his ways. (Matthew 5:48) (NIV) When we strive to be perfect, is not that we just want to be perfect but our Father wants us to be perfect as He is. At the sounding of the trumpet, the saints will have their physical bodies, as they resurrect, they are united with their soul or spirit they will be glorified and. Instead of having a physical body, it will be a spiritual being of the saints this will last eternity.

1 Corinthians chapter 15 teaches about the resurrected bodies

that they will be; Although the physical body was corrupted by the devil, it will be an uncorrupted spiritual being well glorified, before it had some weaknesses, but will rise in power. It is better always to strive to do good striving for excellence without being jealousy with others is a healthy thing to do, especially if we are doing it in the name of the Lord so that His name is glorified. If we are striving to be perfect it means we are striving to be saints which is a good thing. To be a saint we must always strive to do good because what the Lord is looking forward for us to do although we are fighting against forces of darkness, it better to keep on trying to do good because that is what the Lord wants us to do and He will be glorified with that. When we are perfect, we must struggle to maintain that standard. This must be maintained because heavenly beings are perfect. Jesus sacrificed His blood on the cross for us to be perfect and for us to be saved.

Keep the Kingdom of Heaven is Separate from Politics

Our citizenship to the heavenly kingdom means that we have a duty to be loyal to Christ. There are so many reasons why we should learn to keep the kingdom of God separate from politics. (2 Corinthians 4:4) (NIV) (1 John 5:19) (NIV) (Luke 4:6) (NIV) We are warned to be careful when we are pursuing the worldly wealth, because the devil has said that it belongs to him. (Romans 13) (NIV) We have to cooperate with governing authorities but we should always note that there is a very thin dividing line that we would end up mixing the heavenly authority and the earthly authority. So we have to obey the governing authorities with caution if we are to avoid contamination. The problem that mostly arises is that, although you may start well, but somewhere along the line the devil may find a way and get in and start influencing you and slowly you may get carried away. Jesus kept on in insisting that his kingdom was not of this world, so if we are following Him, we have to make sure that we do not end up pursuing two kingdoms, yet there is a contrast between these two kingdoms. The wealth of this world will make us survive, we all need some sort of wealth to be able to live a life on this world, there is a very thin dividing line between accumulating wealth in order to survive and accumulating wealth because you will be led by the devil who wants you to worship him in order for him to give you those riches. No one else will judge for you, but it is only you to judge for yourself, you are now caught in between, accepting wealth from the devil which is worldly or accepting the true heavenly wealth which is eternal.

If we say we are following Jesus, we must truly follow all His ways which we know that He was offered a kingly crown of the kingship of this world, and many times He refused it. Jesus expects us to emulate every step of Him because He came to set an example of How life should be lived in order for us to get eternal life.

All what we are doing is trying to follow Jesus' footsteps and striving to get eternal life in the end. Jesus came to establish the heavenly kingdom on earth, by the time He was establishing that kingdom there were many political differences, but that could not deter Him from establishing that kingdom which was His mission on earth, we have to be very careful because we might be facing the same situation. During Jesus' time the Jews were under Roman rule, which means sometimes they could be made to do things they never liked to do, so there was much resistance and resentment. So many people were involved in politics wanting Jesus to be involved, but Jesus had His own mission which He refused to be off track.

Christians have to realise that since Jesus went, He commissioned them to take up and complete His mission. They must know that they are leading people to eternal life, as Jesus would say His kingdom was not of this world, so Christians must know that they are representing the heavenly kingdom and bringing the heavenly kingdom on earth. Since we are representing Him, are we able to say the kingdom is among you as Jesus used to say? The mission of Jesus was of loving the people so He became a servant of the people. If we are representing

Jesus, we must love the people as He did, if we become politicians, we will tend to love only the people of our nationality or the people who come from the same region as I do. Who will represent the other, yet all the people are created in the image of God so must be treated as brothers and sisters?

Those Christians who tried to involve or mixing Christianity with politics ended up having more problems than solving those problems. If Christians are involved in politics, they may appear to be succeeding, that is temporal it will not last long because that will be pursuing two contrasting things and wanting to make them one which will not work because before it never worked.

Politics is a master of the world and of the people, yet the church is a servant of the people and should remain like that. We may think that we are doing good to the church, yet we are doing more harm than good to the church. (John 18:36) (NIV) An example of how bad it is to mix politics with the kingdom of heaven is on the trial of Jesus, they falsely accused Him thinking that He was going to take their political power. They were mixing the heavenly kingdom with the earthly kingdom, Jesus had to remind them that His kingdom was not of this world, but they failed to understand Him. That is what we should always be praying for, to be able to differentiate that the heavenly kingdom is a divine kingdom and not to be likened unto the corrupted worldly kingdom. As Jesus came to give an example, He was never involved in anything that interfered with the worldly kingdom He tried to show them how the heavenly kingdom was, but they seemed to be blinded to that and went on to blindly accuse Him of something abstract. We must all know that this kingdom is people's hearts, carries no weapon of war or defence, but spiritually impowered, this kingdom never used force to advance its powers, it is only fighting spiritual forces, its design is not worldly. If we would truthfully follow his example, our world was going to be a good world to live in because we always pray for that when we say, your kingdom come, the prayer would have been answered, yet instead of waiting for the prayer to be answered, it is us who must strive to do what is done in heaven with the help of the Lord. We ask the Lord to lead us into your truth so that what we do is truthful and no falsehood but honest and straightforward without any blemish, we must not be guided by worldly wisdom but divine wisdom, which comes from heaven. Sin is a robber which comes only to rob us of our relationship with our Father in heaven. Jesus stated clearly beyond any doubt, but it appears they blocked their ears, not that they did not hear Him, but only that they wanted to appear like they did not hear it. Jesus always attracted bigger crowds, but never even a single day did He incite them to take up arms, so where did their fear come from? We must ask our Father to fill us with the Holy Spirit so that we can be able to understand Him when He speaks to us of the nature of the kingdom of heaven. More damage was caused to Christianity before because those who were introducing Christianity were holding the Bible and taking people as slaves and at the same time treated them cruelly, so people became confused if the heavenly kingdom does that at all.

Look how Christianity is declining in those first world countries where they mixed Christianity and enslaving people at the same time. We should learn from our past mistakes and try not to repeat because it has opened our eyes and our minds to know that it is damaging to Christianity.

07

Salvation

Is Salvation Without Conditions?

We ought to have faith and to ask for God's grace because salvation is not by works but by faith. Salvation is being saved from your sin and ready for eternal life, and also it is being protected from anything that might harm your soul. Christianity is trying to deliver you from all the forces of darkness which might prevent you from getting eternal life, which is the goal of Christianity. We are all striving to get eternal life in the end, but along the way we meet some resistance from those forces which want to block our way from getting to eternity. Earning salvation is not trying to invent our own ways of doing things but to follow what Jesus gave us as an example, He came to release the oppressed. So, it means we must not oppress other people, He came for the orphans, means we must look after the orphans, and not to look down upon the widows for they never liked to be. Love God with all your mind and all your heart we will earn it by being faithful to Him by His grace and mercy we will be saved. If we obey the scriptures, that will lead us to eternal life. We do not earn salvation by works but by faith, you have to have faith in the word and in Christ. We mean that salvation is a gift from God, a gift (say) is not something that you have worked for, but when given a gift by a friend you have to be thankful and to be grateful, this salvation we have received from our heavenly Father, we have to be faithful rejoice and give praise to Him who gives us this gift of salvation, that gift is not by works. This started long ago when He loved the world to a point of giving his only son who came here to show us the way, when He was going, he said He would not live us comfortless, and He sent us the Holy Spirit who is guiding us. "We become Christians through God's unmerited grace not the result of any effort or ability, intelligent, choice or act of service on our part". In return for this, we have to be obedient and pass on that unmerited love to others, we have to emulate the example we were given, (Ephesians 2:8-9). This scripture teaches us to have faith because salvation is by faith not our works, so by His grace we will be saved. Salvation is a free gift from God who loved us before we could think of doing any works to please Him, we received after genuine repentance and baptism. We know very well that at one time or another you sinned, so it is better to have prayer and repentance, that is, turning from your old way of doing things and start doing what pleases the Lord, (Acts 2:38-40). When we say salvation is a gift from God, it does not come automatically. You are to take care that you do not neglect salvation that can make you to be saved. Salvation, because it comes through faith and recognising the giver of salvation. The best thing to do is when we hear these things, we must try to do them so it becomes our life application, living what we preach, or what we talk, (Hebrews 2:3). We have to be warned and think of the second coming which we must not be caught unawares as if we were not warned to watch out for those dangers ahead of us. (Matthew 19:17) God's laws are not there to be a burden on us, but to have a good relationship with Him and become members of the trinity. He is pure and Holy, so for us to stay near Him we must keep away from sin so as to qualify to be members of the Holy Family. Sometimes we have a misconception that we must be taken as we are not knowing that to stay in a pure family you have also to be pure, sometimes we have broken the laws and have come short for the glory of heaven, sometimes we have a misconception that my sins are lighter than other sins, therefore, I qualify for heaven, all sins make us sinners, therefore we must repent, no repentance leads to death (Romans 3:23). This is giving a clear warning that if wen sin we will drift away from the salvation, yet this salvation is waiting for us if we do good.

When we are asked to repent when we have sinned, it appears we are asked to do a difficult thing yet they are narrow paths that lead to heaven, we seem to take believing in Jesus lightly yet He is the only way to heaven, (Matthew 7:13-14) (NIV). The laws of God give us peace of mind because when we follow them, we will live a perfect life which leads to a good relationship with God, yet a good relationship with God leads to happiness, (James 1:25) (NIV). God's laws are not meant to oppress us but to show that as we ask for holiness, they make us holy and make us like the heavenly subjects who holy. So, that means we will qualify to be in the trinity, which we are all striving to be. If we obey God's laws, they remind us where we are going wrong so we can repent as God loves those who repent for, they will be His children.

Christ Will Come from Heaven to Rule the Nations, (Rev.19:11-15)

It appears we will be taken unawares because we know very well that Jesus came as a lamb to the slaughter and as a servant and forgetting that God said that everything has its own time, then we think that when He comes to rule H will come in that state again yet he will be coming to rule not time for salvation. We have been forewarned, it is not like we have not been told Jesus came with forgiveness, but it will not be all time for forgives that is the reason why He brought this revelation, so that we know there is time for everything

During the Roman Empire, the victorious generals would ride on a white horse, that is why in a divine revelation John saw a prince riding on a white horse meaning that Jesus will come victoriously, taking into account that He was nailed to the cross and all either murdered or persecuted or tormented to death. Christ comes to earth at close of the tribulation, at His first coming He came as a lamb, but this time coming as a victorious king of kings and Lord of lords, (Matthew 25:31-46) (NIV) When it is said the time will come, it appears very remote or very fictitious, that it looks of no value to be taken heed of. Like what happened at the coming of the Messiah people were taken unawares, the same thing is going to happen at the coming of the judgement, we must be warned. What we meet with in our lives everyday appearing like ordinary things are the ones we must take seriously for we will judge of them. How do you feel to find yourself on the wrong side of judgement? The time to be obedient and do the right thing is now, while we still have the time to repent and be saved. We should not be like people who did not learn the scriptures which are telling us what will happen and for us to be alert and try to avoid the coming judgement. (Zechariah 14:1-42) (NIV) Zechariah is warning us that this day is definitely coming, why should we be taken unawares as if the scriptures were not fore warning us, so is saying let us be obedient and do what the scriptures are telling us to do. (Thessalonians 2:7-12) (NIV) We are being warned daily by the scriptures, but there are some evil powers which want to deceive us. We should always ask God to help us to be able to fight against those powers, which want to steal our salvation which the Lord Jesus has brought to us, we deserve it if we obey and have faith. (Hebrews 9:27-28) (NIV) We have been warned enough that as sure as death judgement is as sure as that, the author is appealing to the reader to say let us take heed for now is still His time of love not judgement, but judgement is coming.

08

Citizens of Kingdoms

The Kingdom of the World is Naturally Tribal: (intrinsically)

ometimes when we have known the people who are close to us or those whom we have known before, we tend think that others are our enemies. If we take the story of the good Samaritan, we would learn to treat all humans the same. Tribalism is what is in the kingdom of the world, dominated by advancing and promoting own people or grouping. Apart from promoting its own grouping, it receives bribes and becomes corrupted. Heavily inclined to family tribal and clan. When acquiring land, they want it to belong to the family tribe or clan forgetting all others. This means that you will be taking your tribe as the superior one and looking down upon other tribes as inferior. This sort of doing things will corrupt the earthly kingdom and makes the contrast to be very visible. The way they do things will make them contrast heavily with the heavenly kingdom which takes everyone as equal and taking everything as belonging to our heavenly Father and hence, we are His children so as to be able to inherit whatever our Father has got for us is all Ours. Confessing your sins is to do it or say it with your mouth, you cannot leave it to say the Lord knows my sins without you confessing them. When you recognise your sins, do not try to be intelligent thinking that the Lord does not know everything. Do not try to show your reasoning but to confess whole heartedly admit that you have sinned against the Lord, humble yourself and be bold enough to say I have sinned against you Lord. He is faithful enough to wash away all your sins. This means that the heavenly kingdom takes every human being on equal footing. This present-day could be suffering from what the Israelites suffered when they rejected Jesus Christ as a Messiah. The reason being that as they were oppressed, they were looking for a political Messiah (Jeremiah 23:5) (NIV) Jeremiah was prophesying the coming of the Messiah the perfect king who would not be corrupted with this world. If we follow His example, we will not be corrupted by this world. Jeremiah prophesied the coming of the saviour, He would redeem the children of Israel. These Israelites being under the Roman Rule had high expectations that He would be a political leader, and relieve them from the Roman Rule. To their surprise, He was crucified and died, when He rose from the dead, to their biggest surprise, He ascended to heaven, leaving them under that rule. We must always understand how God works He does not work the way we would expect Him to work, sometimes we are saying He does not answer our prayers. We are saying He hears but, when it comes to answering, He has set His own timetable. (Psalms 48:2) (NIV) They would be excused because when one is oppressed, you tend to want to be liberated there and then. The Israelites expected a worrier Jesus Christ, mixing the heavenly kingdom with the earthly kingdom. Like the Israelites who missed the target, we might miss the target as well, and miss the spiritual deliverance, (John 18:36) (NIV). We seem to be mixing these kingdoms we very much need the earthly power at the same time want the power of the heavenly kingdom. Jesus never took the earthly power and its earthly kingdom, because His kingdom was not of this earth but the heavenly kingdom. We have to be decided on which kingdom we are going to serve, the earthly one or the heavenly one? Pilate could not understand the heavenly kingdom because he did not have revelation.

We pray that we think of the present, and also think of the future so that we can be forewarned of the second coming (Revelation 19:11-13) (NIV). "Because the Lord used the terms "Kingdom of Heaven" and "Kingdom of God" interchangeably in places in the four gospels, most Christians think they are one and the same. They will be, but not until the second coming of the Lord Jesus Christ when He rules the world for a thousand years on the throne of His father David (In the flesh, Jesus was in the bloodline of king David: in His deity, Jesus was begotten by the bloodline of God the Father)"

The Kingdom of Heaven is Centred on Loving

We know it pains, but we should practise love for our neighbours, if we practise that, it will make our life worth living, but only if we ask the Holy Spirit to take charge. (Matthew 16:19) When Jesus told Peter that He was giving Him the keys for heaven and earth, it was not Marely from nowhere, it was after Peter had had been led by the Holy Spirit to say what he had said, so Jesus gave Him the keys, which means as everything was handed down from those disciples to us, it means the keys have been handed down to us, to make this clear, it is not automatically that we have the keys to heaven, it only means we have to stay pure to be given these keys. First, the kingdom must manifest in you because the kingdom of God is within us, that kingdom must not be a kingdom of words but a kingdom of works and faith. What we are all striving for is to lead a God-centred life, which we know a God-centred life is a life of loving, a life of caring. To lead a God-centred life means to worship, to worship means to submit yourself to God who is the creator of all nature. The good thing is that He listens, He is truthful and graceful. When we worship, we should not be self-centred but to humble ourselves. As God created us, that means He loves us, so we must keep as close to Him as we can so we can stay in that Holiness.

The church encourages people to stay in prayer, even Jesus himself said stay in prayer so as to stay connected above and below. Stay in prayer in order to keep that holiness, we have to always be asking for this holiness. Jesus teaches us to always pray and not seizing, He teaches us that to be always praying and not to be repeating our prayer but to stay as close to Him as we can, meaning that where ever you are you must always think of doing good, every person must have a desire to serve the community, do not wait for Sunday, or to wait for a time of prayer, (Luke 18:1-30) (NIV). As we stay in prayer, our God is prepared to listen to our prayers, let us not give up, for the Lord takes His time according to His plans and not according to our plans. God reigns as king in the Spiritual realms, it reigns as the Spiritual kingdom. As the heavenly kingdom is centred on loving, let it filter through to the earthly kingdom because that kingdom is a spiritual kingdom which God reigns as king, so we are always asking for that spiritual real to reign here on earth. The kingdom of heaven was always the centre of Jesus' teaching, so let that rule in your heart first then let it manifest to the world through you. Jesus came to be exemplary because His life was of obedience to God, so He pleads with us to live a life under the authority of the heavenly king because He is the one who has got absolute authority, His laws are not to be debated but be obeyed. A Christian has a certain level of consciousness to always think and search if their names are written in the book of life, we can try by all means to do good works, but best of all is to have faith in in God. Mainly we would say without any hesitation that the coming of Jesus on earth was the coming of the kingdom. God plans His deeds well ahead of time such as at the fall of man, he promised to intervene, but for us because it had taken time so we had forgotten that by the time of the coming of the Messiah, we never believed Him.

The values of the heavenly kingdom are: respecting every human being as they are created in the image of God, love and taking every human being as equals.

1. Faith, brings the benefits of salvation to our lives, which includes healing, prosperity, peace, love, joy, deliverance from demons and curse, sanctification of the mind and emotions, salvation of the soul, which the word of God promises us.

2. Simplicity of a child/purity, Jesus' contrast intellectual pride with child-like simplicity and humility, the simple of heart is like little children in that sense.

3. Belongs to those who suffer, Jesus said, suffer the little children to come unto me which means those who will suffer the little children are blessed.

4. Love God, love your neighbour, "Love the Lord your God with all your heart and with all your soul and with all your mind and with all your strength, and love your neighbour as you love yourself". These two commandments will embody all the ten commandments, to observe them will mean observing all the ten.

5. Honesty/truth, being honest means not telling lies, to be truthful means making known all the full truth of the matter. In courts people are made to hold the Bible and say I will be truthful, but as the proceedings go along, they lie, why?

6. Humility, The Christian tradition unequivocally affirms that humility is a virtue… Jesus talks of humility as the best measure of a person's kingdom readiness. Jesus tells us that we should humble ourselves like little children, we become great in the kingdom of heaven.

7. Joy in others' achievements, being supportive and exhibiting happiness for the success of other people is something everyone should do. We have a very good example of: what we of the earthly kingdom, if we sow a lot, we harvest a lot so, if you are

happy with others a lot, they will be happy us Jesus says. When we say, be happy with what others do, we mean real happiness not just pretending, to be genuine happiness with others can only bring some of the happiness to your soul as well.

8. Wealth and ambitions must be sacrificed, (Matthew 6:24) (NIV) Warning against greed and the desire to earn more money than you could ever spend. If wealth and riches are your ambition, you will never be satisfied. Give to the Lord what He requires of your time, our earthly possessions and our energies to further His work. As the Lord commanded, Seek the kingdom of God, as a priority, because we have to take an example from our father who is perfect, we know it is difficult but we must strive to be like Him. That means, His righteousness and His goodness and everything will be added unto you.

09

The Earthly Kingdom is a tit-for-tat, eye for an eye

(Exodus 21:23-25) (NIV) The law of that time allowed retaliation, but that was found to be primitive, that would mean members of society were allowed to put the law into their own hands, as for now people are not allowed to put the law into their own hands but to leave it to the authorities, and now society will be governed according to the law. Corrected by (Matthew 5:38-42) (NIV) When Jesus was saying if someone slaps you on the cheek, turn to him the other cheek, He did not mean that you should give the other cheek, He meant that you should not seek revenge, we very well know that it pains to be wronged by someone, but we have to ask the Lord to give us the strength and the heart to be able to contain it, yet if the Lord intervenes He makes the burden lighter, and He soothes all pains. Instead of spending your time thinking of how you are going to revenge spend your time thinking of how you are going to mend relation with your neighbour or your friend if you practise that, it will give you maturity in your behaviour, all this will be working towards bringing the kingdom of heaven to earth so when we are talking to the Lord, let us ask Him to use us so that the heavenly kingdom will manifest in us. The reason why the earthly kingdom is tit-for-tat, eye for an eye, if the world would go on with this eye for an eye, were we going to end up with blind people in the world? Who was going to be the one survivor after taking off other people's eyes, it is because the earthly kingdom is mostly dominated by the devil who wants to see the world in dispute or in disarray always?

It appears we still have a long way to go, because if we look at it currently, if one country bombs the other, we are always seeing the other country returning it by bombing as well. Is that not called tit for tat? If it is not, what is it? If the countries are allowed a tit for tat, then the subjects will copy their countries. If they are forbidden to do it physically, then they have taken it under ground. If someone wrongs me then my attitude to them will be that of revenge, and I shall carry that grudge for years if not for life. Is it not time to start on a clean page? We have been preaching that there should not be a tit for tat for ages now that we should be somewhere by now. There is a lot hidden in our hearts, but the bottom line is, we have not made progress towards establishing the reflection of the heavenly kingdom on earth. It has been said time and again that for the heavenly kingdom to come on earth it must manifest from the heart going out ward into the world, but it appears we are still looking for it to come from heaven to this present day.

The devil seems to be dominating the earthly kingdom for now, before the second coming of Christ. The wrong with the tit-for-tat is that it will never end, it is like a war, everyone in a war wants to appear to have conquered, so everyone will always want to fight back which will make it never-ending. So, nothing will have been solved by the tit-for-tat. If it is not a tit-for-tat, it will end there because one will find no one to compete with so the war ends. Mostly these kingdoms of the world are guided by the devil who wants to rule over them. The devil mostly runs the nations of the world and guides their way of doing things. If guided by Jesus' things will always run smoothly. When you are in the devil's territory, he wants you to take the citizenship of that territory so that once you are a citizen, he will leave you and goes on to find new clients, so that his territory may have millions of dwellers. The empires dominated by the devil, are inhabited by those who trust the sword to solve their scores. It is better to let Jesus take control of your life always, and you will see that it will be life where the light prevails all the time. Tit-for-tat, eye for an eye We would not want anyone to mistreat people the way they have mistreated us, but how we would like them to treat us. (Matthew 5:38-39) (NIV) As we are followers of Jesus Christ, we have to follow his example.

As Followers of Christ, let us Help Build the Kingdom by Living Righteously

1. Be happy, what makes the heavenly kingdom happy is the repenting of one sinner than many people who do not need repentance If the heavenly kingdom comes and God's will done on earth, there will always be happiness on earth.
2. be Positive, help to build the kingdom of God on earth by living a righteous life, be always happy and to be positive in whatever you do, pray and study the scriptures daily.
3. Pray and study scriptures daily (John 1:8) (NIV) Christ chose to reflect his light through His followers to an unbelieving world because unbelievers are unable to bear the full blazing glory of His light at first hand. We are reflectors of Christ's light we are there to point them to Christ's light.
4. Repent of sins, repentance means turning away from our sins thus if we turn away from our sins there is no way we can be condemned to death. By repentance we receive the remission of sins for us to receive the gift of the Holy Spirit.
5. Be worth of a temple recommend, we must be morally clean and obey the words of wisdom and we must strive to live a righteous life in order to be worth to live in the holy places of God.

6. Listen to the advice from God, listen to the advice and accept all the requirements of a pure life and you shall avoid being cut off as they do to evil doers, if you search it will be revealed unto you.

7. Love God with all your strength, Love the Lord your God with all your heart, soul and mind, and with all your strength, and love your neighbour as you love yourself.

8. Love your neighbour, loving your neighbour means loving those who are in the community with you and those who are not. Those who live in your neighbourhood and those who are not. Those who work with you, those who go to school with you and those who do not. Those who serve you in your local shops are all your neighbours, so neighbour has got a broader sense so it is not those around your residence but those far and near for one day you will need them.

Jesus' example is never disputed because it can clearly be seen, He was led to the cross without offering any resistance. It is not like Jesus is telling us to do something He would not do himself, what He is asking us to do is what he himself did. We have to know that when we are waiting for an opportunity for vengeance, we are already out of step with the one we are emulating.

The Heavenly Kingdom does not want to Return Evil with Evil

If you return evil with evil, it will go on and on yet when you return evil with good it will create a world of love. Teaching the world love, making the world a good place to live in. (Luke 22-23), These were Jesus' last days on earth so He had to ensure that His mission on earth was accomplished, giving us examples to follow when He is gone. (Exodus 21:23-25) (NIV), we can still see this sort of a thing happening, but now in a hidden way, we can still see a lot of bombing and the other side bombing back. If someone wrongs someone, it may not be exactly a tit-for-tat as such, but a grudge is nursed between the two, tension rises, otherwise having no kind words to each other. Are we really understanding the scriptures and following them, not to say, what will people say if they see me angry and just pretending to be happy, yet the heart is not clean, this should bring us to the understanding that the heart is the Lord's temple? Without waiting for someone to remind us, we should examine ourselves, because it is you and your Lord. Jesus, although He was born of the spirit, He always prayed, staying in touch with His Father. He taught His disciples to always be in prayer so they would not be tempted, He himself was able to overcome temptations as a result of staying in prayer, (Luke 22:53) The power of darkness is always fighting against the Spirit of the Lord because from the start of Jesus' mission on earth up to the cross He met resistance from the powers of darkness. Jesus was saying to His disciples, you are not exempted, to prove this we can see it if we look back as in (Luke 4), we must bear in mind that when the Lord put us on earth, He laid up a path for us, which the devil now wants to lure us away from that path. So, if we are not always in touch with our Heavenly Father, we can easily be taken off track. (1 Peter 5:8) Believers are warned that they are under persecution which they must stay on the alert. The power of darkness is always roaring like a lion seeking to devour anyone found straying. The power of darkness is like an eagle that is very alert looking for an opportunity to pounce on its prey. (Ephesians 6:10-12) We will fight this battle until the end like Jesus who fought the same battle until the cross. Jesus forewarned us that we are not spared, we will always be faced with trying times.

The Earthly Kingdom Has so many Enemies

The earthly kingdom is always fighting earthly battles which are never-ending because the earthly kingdom is established in a corrupt world. That is the reason why it carries the sword, it says, that is for self-defence, yet it never ends, because the other side also wants self-defence, and also carries a sword. Where you want to defend yourself against someone, there is someone who wants to defend themselves against you, so who is enemy number one? Jesus is preaching the kingdom is at hand, how are we going to meet that kingdom with a sword in our hands? For two opposing things to meet, something must happen, it is either we give up our sword or we do not qualify, but our wish is to qualify. If we qualify that means eternal life. The kingdom of God has to be both present and future, for us to qualify for the future we must be living in the present kingdom. This was said to be already with us, so all that we do must show that we are living in the heavenly kingdom.

The Earthly kingdom is Always Fighting Battles

Earthly governments give their reasons for carrying a sword as defending their subjects. You ask individuals, they will tell you they want to defend themselves from individual enemy, while the other individual says the same, so who is defending who from who? They are all finding excuses why can't someone start the peace process then the other side will follow.

It appears when Jesus taught a sermon on the mount, it was all in vain because no one is taking heed of that. no one is prepared to listen to that when Jesus was saying in that sermon, do not retaliate no one listens. (Luke 3:14) (NIV) Even during John the Baptist's time soldiers and police were there when they wanted to know if it was wrong to be in the army or to be in the police force they were told that it was not wrong, but only that they should not overdo their work, but to do it according to the law do not take bribes do not use force because you have the power soldiers and police should be there for the safety of the public, but not to be a problem to society, because in all these organisations we have honest and dishonest people. (John 18:36) (NIV) Jesus stated clearly that He was king but the kingdom was a heavenly kingdom so if we are following Him, it means we will rule with Him in that kingdom. (Romans 13:3-4) (NIV) The people in authority must realise that they are working for the Lord, so they must strive to work according to the requirement of the law if they are unjust then people will fear them and will mistrust them and there is no good relationship. Let us pray for those in authority so that the way they will do their work will enable good understanding and good relationship to be there between them and us.

The Heavenly Kingdom Has no Enemies

(Matthew 6:10) We know that His kingdom will come and rule on earth and establish eternity, but we are saying for now dear Lord transform us and use us as your vessels be in us for now while we are waiting for that day fill us so we can go to all corners of the world so every person will learn to escape before that day comes, when you sent us on the great commission, you promised us that you would be with us, we are asking you to fill us with your Holy Spirit so that we can do your work without fear. We always pray that your kingdom come, meaning that we are longing that the goodness that the kingdom of God has, should come and rule on earth. This is so because we know that He rules with truth, grace, and mercy, in other words, we are saying give us also that grace and mercy so that whatever we do may manifest your kingdom. (1 Thessalonians 5:2-3) It is well known that the day of the Lord, that is, the judgement day will come without any one knowing it. This comes like a thief who comes without anyone knowing because the thief usually come at night when we are sleeping. When we think that there is peace and safety, is when destruction will come on us suddenly, like labour pain on a pregnant woman, and there is no one to escape. There will be a time when God is going to intervene in worldly affairs. This was predicted in the Old Testament in (Isaiah 13:6). The day of the Lord will include both punishment and blessings. Christ will judge sin and set up His rule on earth for a thousand years. The reason why that heavenly kingdom has no enemies is that it is not an enemy to anyone it loves everyone so in return it will also be loved. Let us start practising loving anyone you will see that everyone loves you in return. It is said that the heavenly kingdom has no enemies, yes it loves us, but it is us who run away from it so we become enemies of ourselves not the heavenly kingdom. The war that the heavenly kingdom faces is not a war of fighting with tangible equipment like what is done on earth, because it is not a war of flesh and blood, but fighting the powers of darkness, which we should wear a spiritual armour. (Ephesians 6:12) (NIV) we must always pray for spiritual strength in order to be able to fight the powers of darkness which are not seen, forces of evil spirits and powers of darkness and all forces of evil.

10

Your Gospel and my Gospel

Romans 2:16), As we pray, let us bear in mind that whatever we do, the way we do it we will not end up making it our god. For example, wealth is good for our living but the way we look for it should give us time to talk to the Lord or to do some work for Him. You submit to sin in such a way that in the end you become a slave of sin. Be obedient to the work of God in such a way that if you become a slave, you will be a slave of the highest. The scripture says that on the day all our secretes will be revealed (Romans 16:25) We are expected not to be taken unawares because everything has been put to us and everything has been explained so we will have no excuse (Ephesians 6:19) We must avoid speaking what we want as if we were working in our own fields, yet we must ask Him to guide us and reveal what He wants to be given to His people. Sometimes we meet with some resistance and face difficult times as if He is not there, we must pre empty ourselves knowing that He does His things according to His will. (Romans 10:16) We must not be down hearted if our message appears not received, even those who came before us not all their preaching was accepted, even Jesus sometimes He met with some resistance. We must not lose heart because there are some lost souls there waiting to be saved by our word. (NIV)The problem we are faced with these days is that people are using the Bible to accomplish their different motives. As a result, the gospel is diluted, it is no more as spiritually centred as it was, should we carry on like that and expect things to shape themselves? We should humble ourselves and ask the Lord to fill us with His Holy Spirit, because it is easy to drift, and become a fake prophet. As we spread the gospel, we must bear in mind that the motive is to save souls, we have to bear in mind that there is someone evaluating all what we are doing, how do you value what you are doing, each time we are trying to interpret the scriptures, we must interpret them as they really mean always bearing in mind that we are trying to save people from going to hell. We have to bear it that there are so many who are interpreting it differently which may end up in leading people astray. As we want to save people from going to hell, we must always pray to be given the true meaning of the scriptures so as to feed the people with the true gospel which saves people from going to hell. This is not an easy task but a task of giving people a choice of either going to hell or spending life in eternity.

We must bear in mind that we must always be guided by the Holy Spirit to be effective and feed the people with a live spiritual gospel. Jesus did not mince His words, He said, teach them what I have commanded you which means He wants us to do exactly as He was doing it not our own way that please our flesh, but even if it means sacrificing our lives, He also sacrificed His life so let it be on us because we are His followers, not pretenders.

Let us ask the Lord to Guide us

The Lord through the Holy Spirit will guide us to do things truthfully, and according to how they should be done. The Lord Himself promised to guide us, sometimes we have our own needs, we have to ask Him in faith to grant us those needs. He is faithful and honest enough to meet all our needs, so that we are not found wanting. We must always look to Him for guidance, He is our shepherd, He is a good shepherd who always led His sheep to greener pastures. The book of life teaches us that His plans are always of leading us to joy and contentment. To keep our relationship, we must always be talking to Him in prayer. If we could ask for anything, but most of all we must ask for wisdom from Him. That means with wisdom we will always be guided to do things that please Him. Sometimes we tend to go ahead of His plans, it is better to let Him lead and we follow. Sometimes we forget and start relying on our own understanding, leaving our Lord behind. If anything, we must ask for the guidance of the Holy Spirit, without any hesitation because this was promised to us by Jesus Himself, so Holy Spirit has to be with us all our lives.

The Lord put everything in His word through the scriptures in order to guide us so whatever we want from him it is there in the scriptures. So, we have to ask Him in good faith knowing that it is His promise to us it is our right to have them, but it does not necessarily mean that we will have to take them without asking for them. We should politely ask for these things from Him, He is the Father we are the sons and daughters that is how our relationship is. His plans to us are to make us joy and to guide us through green pastures, because He wants to see us prosper. God provides wisdom to us so we have to trust in Him to do good for us because His love came before we would ask Him for it.

We very well know that we are guided by the Holy Spirit we must trust the Holy Spirit will not leave us as orphans, to have good guidance we have to surrender ourselves to the Holy Spirit.

The Lord will reveal what He wants to be given to His People

The Lord reveals to us all what He wants through the Holy Spirit, because He loves us, so He wants us to know Him so that our relationship will be a good relationship. (Psalms 25:4-5) (NIV) As we pray to God for guidance, we have to realise that He has already put some of the answers in His word in the scriptures, we must consult the scriptures asking to be guided by the Holy Spirit so that we understand what the Lord says to us through His word. If we are guided by the Holy Spirit, He will teach us to be obedient, if we are obedient, that means we will be able to put into life application what we have learnt. Although we pray, we must ask the Lord to teach us how to pray, we know that a guided prayer is a holy one. If our prayer is guided by Him, it means it is a prayer that will not offend Him. We still have to discover God; we have not known Him yet.

The reason why we should ask for His guidance in prayer is that there is something that the Lord expects from us. Sometimes we do our own while He has His expectations, there are times we have to model our prayers on His Son's prayer. The Son said, He wanted something done, but let your will be done. We must give everything to Him so that we are doing His will in the end.

Once His will is done on us, that means we will be doing things according to His will.

Our Lord is good to us because He keeps all His promises to us, whatever He said He would do for, He will do. They cannot always speak to us in the same ways as He did before, but He put all His ways in the Bible. Sometimes we are stark not knowing what to do, as we pray sometimes it becomes very clear what to do or what to follow. The good thing is, the Lord keeps His promise, His is not like us for we are inconsistent.

We must always pray that the Holy Spirit be with us all the time so that we see His presence, because He is always present but we do not see it, open our eyes so that we see you, Lord. The Lord wants us to know Him so He reveals Himself to us in so many different ways. Sometimes we can see Him through His creation, we have to see and know how He is through His creation. God communicates with us through so many different ways, which we have to learn and know Him from there, God is love to us.

Lord, Let Your Will be Done

If God's will be done on earth as it is in heaven, it will mean that the earth will be an interesting place to live in. (Matthew 6:10) (NIV) we know that you can set up your kingdom on earth as it is in heaven through us.

Whatever might want to prevent us from doing the will of God here on earth, I pray that it be accomplished. There are so many forces that want to prevent us from doing the will of God, these forces are not as powerful as our Lord, always His will should prevail. Sometimes we go against the will of God because of lack of knowledge, not knowing that everything is His even myself I belong to Him. Why should I do like I am redirecting Him on what to do, we have to abide by His will, let your will be done on earth and on everyone.

We must always be asking the Lord to use us as He wishes knowing that if His will is done on us, He will keep us in good shape, because He will have moulded us the way we should be. We want to be your vessels so that we are usable for the work of the Lord. (Mark 14:36) (NIV) Sometimes some situations that we dread them and start doing our will not knowing that by doing that we are doing our own will not the will of the Lord, instead of saying your will be done on me so that you can use me as you like. (Luke 22:42) (NIV) In life we are sometimes faced with situations that will make us dread, but the Lord sees and knows everything that we face, it is better to ask Him to strengthen us, and to ask Him to let His will to be done, then if his will is done on us then we preparing for eternal life, because that is our goal. Jesus gave us a very good example which we must follow, in order to get eternal life. (Romans 8:28-29) (NIV) Sometimes God called us and predestined us but at the same time we have to go through some hard and trying times, which we have to endure, and to remember to put Him in the front of all our deeds, it may appear difficult and unsurmountable but we have to persevere in the end the Lord's will, should be done. Sometimes we may forget and start thinking that we can do them on our own, but this is not the case, let your will be done, Jesus taught us like this: "Father, if you are willing, take this cup from me; yet not my will, but yours be done." Most of the times we tend to go ahead of the Lord, yet He has plans for us.

On Judgement Day, all our Secrets Will be Revealed

The purpose of the judgement day is to put everything that we did in front of the one who will be judging so that the decision will be made. (Luke 8:17) (NIV) What we are doing as preachers is to reveal the light of the Lord to the people because that is what he said when He commissioned His disciples to make everyone see the light of the Lord so that when the time comes there will be no excuse from anybody that they did not know anything about the light of the Lord, what we are witnessing about Christ to them must be clear so that no one is left in doubt. There are so many people out there who require to see the light of Christ, if this light is revealed to us we must impart it to them so that everyone sees this light (Matthew 10:26) (NIV) When Jesus was preparing His disciples, He knew what would happen in future, He assured everyone which was handed down to us knowing that we may be falsely accused He said do not fear for nothing will stay hidden for ever, following to what happened to Jesus, it might happen to us knowing that we are following in His footsteps. Sometimes we delude ourselves thinking that no one is seeing me therefore I can do things that are not pleasing to the Lord, yet a day is coming when everything will be clearly displayed.

Let us not try to hide anything, for there is someone who is seeing everything we are doing and the way we are doing it. We think we are hiding, there is someone who sees and knows everything that we might think we are hiding. Nor should we judge others for there is one who judges all. (2 Corinthians 5:10) (NIV) We always say, we are saved by faith and not by our works there shall still be a judgement day when all what we did will be brought for judgement then we will be rewarded according what we did. (1 Corinthians 4:5) (NIV) One sin we might be committing we who are supposed to bring light to the people, is when we start judging instead of bringing the light of Christ to them, it is not for to find out whether people are good or bad. The reason why we should leave everything to Him is because He is the one who knows the heart of a person so He is the one who has the right judgement we cannot say who is a better servant for Christ. When we are judging, that means we are taking ourselves as better than them, yet that is not true, we always say we cannot judge, but there is one who will judge and is the one who knows everything and knows every sin of ours, what we can only do as preachers is to tell people that we should stay pure and to obey His commandments. What we tell people is that everything will be brought to light on that day what we are saying is that there will be nothing to hide and nowhere to hide, each one and not as a group will receive their judgement (Luke 12:2-3) (NIV) Sometimes we pretend to be holier than other when it is only hypocrisy. It is not right to pretend to people that we are perfect when we are not. Instead, what we should do is to ask God to perfect us, give us a good heart so that what we do we do it in truth and in spirit. Pray to the Lord to take away all untruthfulness and serve the Lord whole heartedly. Jesus clearly pointed it out that that whatever we did in any privacy even what I whispered into someone's ear. We as Christians we may be chasing away many would be Christians, but by our hypocrisy we chased them away. They will be giving our hypocrisy as an excuse, let us try to be perfect and not pretend, let us admit that we are not perfect and ask the Lord to help us, otherwise we need His grace and mercy.

We are Working in the Lord's Field

Those who work in God's vineyard will get a reward, so, let us work in that vine yard happily and honestly knowing that we will get a reward. (1 Corinthians 3:9) (NIV) We are God's fellow workers in

God's field, the Lord Jesus when He knew He was about to go, He did not just go, but He gave us some assignment. This shows how much He wants us to work in His field, the Lord wants us to labour for Him, besides seeing us labour for Him He wants to dwell in us we are His temple, let us look after His temple. If we miss use His temple, we will give an account in the end. God has given us so many different talents knowing that there is a lot of different tasks to be carried on in His field Let us not ask to have someone's gift yet He wants to use those gifts that He has given us. Sometimes we tend to want someone's gift because we want glory for ourselves yet all the glory must go to Him. We are God's people whatever we do the people of the Lord, we are working in the Lord's field. The world is to be evangelised not by miracles but by the deeds of every person, whatever we do we must know that we are working for the Lord. So, we must do it knowing that we are not doing it to please anybody, but it is for the Lord who sees everybody all the time. Many times, we forget and start thinking that it is our field and start behaving that way yet the Lord sees all what we do and He judges every man according to their deeds. That is why we always advise that let Him lead and we follow. It makes sense when He leads because that will mean He is doing His will, we need to cooperate with the owner of the field.

Be Guided by the Holy Spirit

The work of the Holy Spirit in us is to make us know what is good, or what is bed so we have to obey the Holy Spirit because it guides us to do good all the time. Besides comforting us, the Holy Spirit gives us strength where we are becoming weak, sometimes we become weak and very vulnerable in Christian journey. God knew we would encounter such times that is why He gave us the Holy Spirit to strengthen us and to give us power. The Holy Spirit gives us strength to preach the word of God and to share the good news with others. It strengthens us to stand firm for Christ in trials and temptations, forgive others and live a holy life. The Holy Spirit strengthen the body of Christ by giving different gifts to His people. Even if we do not know how to pray the Holy Spirit will help us and gives us words to say, it is interesting to note that God is always present in us through the Holy Spirit. At times we do not know what God wants us to pray for, but the Holy Spirit prays for us with groaning that cannot be expressed in words. Holy Spirit helps us in our weakness, for we may not know what to pray for as we ought to but the Spirit himself intercedes for us with groaning too deep for words. With the help of the Holy Spirit, although we were supposed to be inferior, it exalts us to the level of the apostles who did great works of God during their time. When we seek the hidden things of God, Holy Spirit gives us a revelation, will reveal to us the gifts and talents we have so that we can use it for the work of God. He reveals to us those who are in need so that we can help, He should give us a heart to know that there are some people who are in need, so we should not be selfish. Let us allow Holy Spirit to fill us in such a way that we will be flooded with the Spirit such that I will receive what God wants. As people who know what God wants, we now know that we are poor in spirit so we keep on asking God to fill us so that we can, be able to do the work of the Lord without any fear. Blessed are they who mourn for they shall be filled means that as we know that we are not perfect we ask the Lord to fill us so that we can be up to be what is required to be spiritually. As we search for God in our lives, Please Holy Spirit intercede for us help us to search for God in our lives, sometimes the Holy Spirit prays for us when we do not know, we should strive to know what the Holy Spirit is doing on our behalf, by what is done by the Holy Spirit God knows what we want and when we want it, we should be grateful for that, love Him and give all the glory to Him all the time of our lives. My flesh and my heart may fail, but God is the strength of my heart and my portion for ever. God will provide strength even if our bodies cannot and long after we gone. My strength should not lean on worldly things that will rust and perish but lean on God who is my strength and my fortress in times of need, He will not fail me. God can do great things by using people the way He wants because everything is His so He can use them the way He wants and what He wants at the time He wants. Be strong and courageous; do not be frightened and do not be dismayed for the Lord your God is with you wherever you go. He has always been, God is my salvation; I will trust and do not be afraid He has always been my strength and will always be my salvation for evermore. I will be happy about my weakness because I know that He is my strength because I know that Christ's power lives in me all the days of my life. When I do things for Christ even if I know that they will be too hard for me I know the Lord will be with me. so let us perform our work with some holiness knowing that the Lord is dwelling in us all the time. (Acts 10:37-38) (NIV) Everything we do must be guided by the Holy Spirit otherwise we are doing things using our flesh and blood, when we are witnessing for Christ, we must always ask for the guidance of the Holy Spirit, knowing that Jesus although He was bone of the spirit He always prayed to God for the Holy Spirit. You also know that during the persecution of the apostles, they performed wonders because they were led by the holy spirit. This was promised by Jesus that when the Holy Spirit comes, He will guide you into the truth, and also Jesus made us know that what the Holy Spirit does is in agreement with the other members of the trinity. The Holy Spirit will make us know of the heavenly things which when we know them, we are preparing for eternal life. He will reveal everything that is good for us and will make our relationship between the Father and us a good relationship. The Holy Spirit will make us obey God's commandments.

Since we cannot do anything on our own, we have to trust the Holy Spirit to lead us and guide us in order for us to stay pure and righteous which is what our Father in heaven requires us to be. The Holy Spirit reveals to us the hidden things of the heaven, will help us to observe them, by observing them it will give us a good relationship with our Father in heaven. To be guided by the Holy Spirit must not be a one-day thing or a thing of the past, but must be our daily application and we must ask Him to be with us all the time. Holy Spirit cannot come on His own, but we have to ask Him to be with us and will be very happy to be invited into our hearts.

The disciples of Jesus set a very good example for us, because before they received the Holy Spirit, they could not do anything on their own, but after receiving the Holy Spirit, they were fearless, able to take God's word all over the world that even those who were in darkness can now see the light of God.

11

Christianity and Religion

hristianity is the only religion where God is born as a man, becomes fully human, this shows the height of enlightenment to mankind, all other religions say man must work their way towards divinity. Christianity has become the world religion with more than 2.38 billion followers. The Christian faith is based on the belief that there is birth, life, death, and resurrection of Christ, with that belief could be the reason why it is the most practised in the world. Christianity is followed by Islam, they are like this: Christianity 2.38 billion, Islam 1.9 billion. Christianity started in the first century when Jesus who was born of a Jewish family, did very wonderful works, He had some followers who walked with Him daily for three years. He did not start a religion, by the time He died, His followers continued the work that He had started, they did it exactly as Christ was doing it. They were said to be like Christ, then Christianity started growing from there and became a world religion. This religion believes that there is God and that He must be given all the glory and must be revered.

Hinduism Religion is said to be the Oldest of all the religions, but according to the number of followers, they can be classified as: Christianity first, Islam second, and Hinduism third, its followers are mostly of Indian origin. In Christianity, they believe for sure that Jesus is the Son of God and that He is second in the trinity, when He came to earth, He was the one who was prophesied that there would come a Messiah, He was the promised Messiah.

God's personal reign on earth

During the time for His judgement, God will rule for a thousand years, this is called the Millennial Kingdom (Revelations 20:2-7) (NIV) (Genesis 12:1-3) (NIV) (Luke 1:32-33) (NIV) This is the rule of Christ when He will be ruling in peace, no wars like we are seeing today. Wars will be things of the past there will always be happiness respect for each other. The world is corrupted by the devil who will then be bound for those thousand, let us pray to be able to see that day, and all the happiness that will be there.

Jesus came for the oppressed

Whoever oppresses a poor man insults his Maker, in the earthly kingdom, the poor are being exploited by those who are rich using their wealth to oppress the orphans, the widows and the poor, but he who is generous to the needy honours him, and shall be rewarded. For the needy shall not always be forgotten, and the hope of the poor shall not perish forever. The Bible says help the needy, the poor and the orphans and the widows, but we seem to be doing the opposite, which shows that this world is being ruled by the devil (Psalms 9:7-10) (NIV) The Lord reigns forever, He has established His throne for judgement. He rules the world in righteousness and judges the people with equity. Yet we are asked to seek His kingdom and His righteousness for there is always righteousness in heaven which we are always longing for. What is required of us Christians is for us to try by all means to be that righteous so that we can transform the world, that is what is required of us Christians. The Lord is a refuge for the oppressed, a stronghold in times of trouble. Those who know your name trust in you, for you, Lord you have never forsaken those who seek you. In this life, we may face injustices, we may be falsely accused and misunderstood by friends and enemies, we may not be truly appreciated by others for the love we show, the true value of our work and service may not be duly rewarded. Our ideas may be ignored, but God is to be praised, for He sees and remembers every good we do, and it is up to Him to decide the timing and the appropriateness of our rewards. If we do not trust Him to vindicate us, then we will be susceptible to hatred and self-pity. If we do trust Him, we can experience God's peace, we can be free from the worry of how others perceive us and treat us. God will never forsake those who seek Him. Seeking Him means seeking Him in truth and in spirit and not only seeking Him for the sake of seeking Him. To forsake someone is to abandon the person. God's promise does not mean that if we trust Him, we will escape loss or suffering: it means that God Himself will never leave us no matter what we face. It is said, sometimes we meet situations which appear like God is not on our side, yet God will never forsake us because His love to us is great. This love came to us before we asked for it, this love must be reciprocated. But the needy will not always be forgotten, nor the hope of the afflicted ever perish.

In the first century of Christianity, it appears people were more sympathetic to the poor than we are today, because they used to clothe them and give them something to eat more than we are doing today. The poor were fed, clothed, and sheltered at a personal sacrifice, and the pagans say about Christians: See how they love each other.

Today the poor are being fed clothed and sheltered by the politicians who use taxpayers to do what the Christians are supposed to be doing.

And because the poor are no longer fed, clothed, and sheltered as personal sacrifice, but at taxpayers' expense, pagans say about Christians: See how they pass their responsibility to the tax payer.

Christian service: Serving others and seeking social Justice, real religion the kind that God the Father wants us to be. This religion should reach out to the homeless and loveless in their plight to alleviate their suffering, and guard against corruption, from the Godless world. (James 1:27), religion that God our Father accepts as pure and faultless is this, look after orphans and widows in their distress.

Jesus came for the poor and those without Hope

It is not good for us to only say Jesus was good to the oppressed, instead let us ask Him to give us the Holy Spirit which will enable us to do the same, if the Holy Spirit is with us we can also do it. We should follow the way Jesus did, He loved the poor and showed us how to care for the oppressed. Let us all strive to do the same as we follow His example, we should pray for children and their families and all the communities that are in need. (Deuteronomy 26:6-9) (NIV), as Christians, we should learn not to mistreat other people especially the poor and the children because they are all your people, you hear them when they cry to you. (Job 5:15-16) (NIV), people seem to take advantage of the poor, which should not be the case, yet we should do all we can to help them instead. Lord since we are representing you here on earth, make us love the poor, not only loving them, make us to be able to help them, give us a heart for them. (Luke 4:17-19) (NIV) Lord, we ask you in prayer that you open our spiritual eyes and spiritual minds that we know your mission here on earth. We want to represent you here on earth, that is what you commissioned us to do, our wish is to do exactly as you want us to do, please guide us with your Holy Spirit as you said you would be with us. As you gave us the authority, you promised to be with us as we do your work. You spoke of the present and the future, make us able to work for the present and work for the future knowing that we still have to give a report, so be with us as we strive to do your will, to love the children, the widows and the poor. (James 2:5) (NIV) Lord give us a heart to know that the riches of this world can make us to be far from you depending on how we use them to advance your kingdom, with this earthly wealth we can use it to promote your kingdom or use it to oppress the poor and the marginalised depending on the way we are using that wealth. Make us realise that it is not poverty that will automatically take us to heaven, but it is the way we take you into our hearts, knowing that you are our saviour. The rich can go to heaven providing they are using the wealth they have to promote the kingdom of heaven on earth because that is what you want, we can do your will when you are with us as you promised to be with us all the way. We have the greatest need for salvation, make us know that what we are working for is salvation whether we are rich or poor, if we are rich take the pride away from us, if we are poor, make us realise that it is not poverty that will automatically take us to heaven, but to have faith and accept you as our saviour. May the Lord guide us so that we do not rob the oppressed, instead we have a heart to help them to make sure all injustice is removed from them, make us live in humility and gratefulness.

The earthly Subjects Should Emulate Jesus

We must strive and emulate Jesus because that is the way we can honour God, because He himself honoured us first and gave us His Son doing all that for our salvation that is why we should emulate what Jesus did here on earth because that was done for us. There are so many earthly desires which we must try to weigh against the needy, children copy their parents, so if we are the children of God, let us copy our parents, children who stay close to their parents are loved by their parents because parents say they want very much to be like us. By emulating all His deeds that means that we very much like to be like Him, which means we love heavenly things (Ephesians 5:1-2) (NIV) The author is pleading with the reader that let imitate

God that is, let us learn all His ways, and all about Him. If you are told about a person, you must try learn more about that person so that you get as closer to them as you can. It may appear to be very difficult to imitate Him fully because He was born of the spirit, but He asked us to fear no evil because the Holy Spirit is poured on us, what we can ask Him to do is to keep us filled so can do like Him. Imitating Him means where it is said God is love that means we will be loving like Him, they even say "God is Love" (John 15:14) If we imitate Him fully, the world will be a good place to live in. Let us not end half way, when we mean emulating Him, we mean everything He did, He says whoever wants to follow me must take up his cross and follow me, this does not mean following Him half way, it means taking up your cross and follow Him to calvary.

Look After Yourself that you do not get Polluted by the World

(James 1:27) (NIV), some of the things of the world are so attractive that we get hooked, and so we are corrupted, yet we should be mindful not to be corrupted. Our Father who is in heaven requires us to be fault less and to be pure, we become pure when we obey his instructions, like He wants us to look after His orphans, but we seem to be reluctant. Look after the widows and in general, look after yourself that you do not get polluted by the world, to look after yourself that you do not get polluted, is not to look at just a few things and forgetting that there are so many that can defile you. Have you ever imagined that you have to look after your tongue, that it should not offend anyone? That what we want to take as the least but it will make us very unclean because if you do not control your tongue, you should know that you are offending other people through your tongue. Look after the words that come out of your mouth, have you done an audit of them? It is lying to the Lord to say that I am pure when your words have chased many from the church. What about your deeds, are the pure that others would like to copy that, what are people going to emulate on you that you would say to the Lord I have brought some souls to you because people liked to be as you are, the harvest is plentiful but the labourers are few in the Lord's field. Have you not been polluted by the world yet that you are still worshipping the true God, have you not been carried away that you are now worshipping idols? Worshipping idols is not something tangible that you could see that I am now worshipping idols, you may drift without knowing it that when you look back you will see that you have drifted very far. Wealth is good for us all, but the way you may looking for it may end in you worshipping idols without you knowing it. To be pure in the eyes of God is not to be looking at one or two things only, like looking after the orphans or looking after the widows only but they are so many, you must be able to accomplish them all if you are to be pure in the eyes of God.

In Christianity there are morals and ethics that are to be followed like in every walk of life, they seem not easy to follow like in every walk of life they need commitment on our part to be able to overcome them. The world is full of riches which are not all of them Godly, so it is for us to keep ourselves focused on the true God. The values of the world are based on money, power, and pleasure: money is important in our lives, but let us know that the way we look for it, we must not end up abusing the use of it and to leave us with no time to do the will of God. We have to be reminded that when Jesus was being tempted, He was shown the riches of the world. Are we going to have some boundaries when we are chasing worldly riches? When we seek worldly power, we will get to a stage where we will be power-hungry in such a way that we will not want to relinquish that power, that you want to hold on to that power at any cost even if it means costing someone's life you do not care as long as you have the power. Most of the things in the world are very enjoyable that when we are involved in them, seem to make us happy and will make us forget that there is God, that is how pleasure is. All these things we have mentioned, have no limit, we have to limit ourselves so that we are not corrupted with them. So, we have to be careful when we are pursuing the values of this world. How do we care for the poor? How are we going to provide for the hungry? What are we to do about the marginalised who are treated unjustly? Here are instructions from the Bible. Use a phrase from one of the following scriptures as a slogan to promote helping others:

The Lord asked us not to take advantage of a widow or an orphan: (Exodus 22:22) (NIV): What happened to them is not something of their choice, but that it only happened whether they liked it or not. The Lord will not hesitate to punish their oppressors. Be forewarned and not to wait for the wrath of the Lord to fall on you as if you were walking blindly. Let us ask God to give us the heart to be able to sympathise with them, since they have no power or someone to stand for them, we seem to take advantage of them, yet if God gives us the heart, we will take them as equals to us and treat them as ourselves. For us to take advantage of them, we are putting fire on ourselves because God's eye is on them. If we are helping them, we are doing the will of God, then He will reward us for that instead of cursing us.

Matthew 19:21; Jesus told the rich young man that if he wanted to be perfect, must go and sell all his possessions, and give to the poor, and he would have treasure in heaven. For us to be told that you will have treasure in heaven, appears very remote for us. Jesus advised him that, after selling his possession and ging the money to the poor, he should follow him. Jesus wants us to be self-sufficient so that we are able to look after ourselves so that we are not a burden to others. Jesus was actually saying, we should try by all means to look after the poor. All these things are in His power, to give us a heart, and to provide us to be able to sustain ourselves and them. Let us not cheat, when we are given let us think of the less privileged and give generously to the ability of what we can, so as to keep our relationship with Him. Matthew 25:35; "For I was hungry and you gave me something to eat, I was thirsty and you gave me something to drink, I was a stranger and you invited me in." I needed clothes and you clothed me, I was sick and you looked after me, I was in prison and you visited me." We meet these things in our daily lives, the problem we are now facing is that we have these things daily such that we are just brushing them aside not even seeing the Lord in them. You would not think for a moment that a person you meet in the street would ever be said you have met Jesus, God helps us. A person you have been seeing and you know that person very well, one day is in hospital, to be turned around and be said Jesus was in the hospital, we pray that we see Jesus in those small things unexpected, a person is in prison, we do not pay a visit, who are we to judge? Let us give God His authority, for we are all His subjects, we are just living through His grace and mercy. All these things mentioned, do not need us to be wealthy, they are acts of goodwill on our part. My brothers and sisters in Christ, we have no excuse as to why we are found lacking. They are simple acts freely given and freely received; we must implement them freely. Yes, the church and the government are doing their part, let us do our part, do not wait for the church, do not wait for the government, the onus is on us, to do what we were commissioned to do He promised to be with us, we cannot walk alone. (Luke 4:18); Jesus said that the anointing of the Lord was upon Him, as a result of that anointing, the Spirit of the Lord was upon Him, as a result of that anointing He was proclaiming good news to the poor, freedom for prisoners recovery of sight to the blind, and to set the oppressed free. To proclaim the year of the Lord and the year of jubilee to the slaves. Jesus was quoting from (Isaiah 61:1-2), Isaiah was talking of the release from exile in Babylon of the Israelites, as a year of jubilee when all debts are cancelled, all slaves are set free and all property is returned to the original owners. But the release from Babylon had not brought the expected fulfilment: they were still a conquered and oppressed people. So, Isaiah must have been referring to a future Messianic age, so when Jesus announced that: that day, that scripture was fulfilled in their hearing, Jesus was claiming that He was the one who would bring good news to pass but would do it in a way that the people were not able to grasp. It is good at this moment to remind the reader this process is ongoing. Luke 12:33; Sell your possessions and give to the poor. Provide purses for yourself that will not wear out, a treasure in heaven, that will never fail, where no thief comes near and no moth destroys. Money appears to be everything in our lives, but we have to receive that with caution because it makes our relationship with God to be a distant relationship, and also there will be no connection with the needy. If our relationship with God is a good relationship, He will always provide us with enough for ourselves and the needy.

How Much of my Money am I Going to use for God's Purpose?

we must always strive to use our money for God's work, because whatever He gives us, He is expecting us to honour our part of the agreement. We cannot tell Him to honour His part, because He does. Money should free us to be able to help others, that pleases our Lord. Even in our places of work, there is a system known as "Pay as you earn." If we can do that with worldly things, we should do the same with Godly things because He owns everything. Acts 9:36-42; "In Joppa, there was a disciple named Tabitha (in Greek her name is Dorcas); she was always doing good and helping the poor. About that time, she became sick and died, and her body was washed and placed in an upstairs room. Lydia was near Joppa, so when the disciples heard that Peter was in Lydda, the disciples sent two men to him, and urged him, 'Please come at once!' Peter went with them and when he arrived, he was taken upstairs to the room. All the widows stood around him crying and showing him the robes and other clothes that Dorcas had made while she was still with them. Peter sent them all out of the room; then he got down on his knees and prayed. Turning towards the dead woman, he said, 'Tabitha gets up!' She opened her eyes and seeing Peter she sat up. He took her by the hand and helped her to her feet. Then he called for the believers, especially the widows, and presented her to them alive. This became known all over Joppa, and many people believed in the Lord." When we do good, it may not be known immediately, we have a problem sometimes that we want to make a name for ourselves, yet Dorcas made an impact on her community without knowing it. We should always be doing good to the poor and the marginalised, for that is where Christ's eye is always. A big tree is measured when it is fallen, Dorcas' good works came out on the day she had passed away.

God Uses People to do What He Wants to do on Earth

God also gives His gifts to so many different people. We fall into a trap that we want to have the gifts that others have which may not be our gifts. Let us ask the Lord to make us use the gifts that He has given us to the fullest extent, and the name of the Lord may be lifted up because everything we do is for the glory of the Lord. (Acts 10:4) (NIV) Cornelius stared at him in fear, "What is it Lord?" he asked. The angel answered, that his prayers and his gifts to the poor have come up as a memorial offering before God." We must not expect God to speak to us in the same way He spoke to Moses, to Samuel, to Ruth, or to Cornelius, but He comes to us in so many different ways, what we have to do is to understand the Lord when He comes to us, sometimes He is coming to us in our lives but we are failing to recognise Him, if it is like that then we miss Him. My dear reader, pray to Him so that you do not miss Him if He comes to you. Sometimes it could be once in your life. Stay in prayer so that you recognise Him when He comes. Remember that God may come to you through the people we are interacting with every day so that you will never expect that to be an angel sent to you. You cannot choose for God who to send to you, accept what He has sent to you or who He has sent to you, it might be through circumstances and events, let us stay alert of what God is going to say to us at His own time, not our time if we want to make it our time, we miss out. (Matthew 25): Should we be more focused on saving souls or meeting people's physical needs? Jesus did both, cared deeply about the poor and the downtrodden.

12

Jesus Loves the Orphans and the Widows

Sometimes we forget that when we are able, we have no control over it, and those who are unable did not like it to be like that. If we start thinking in those lines, we will be doing the will of God. It is everyone's responsibility to ensure that the wrongs of social injustice are put right this happens when you see that you are doing what is right yourself. Please represent those who cannot do it for themselves, do not just keep quiet when there is something that is unjust to those who cannot help, stand for themselves. Luke 4:18 says it as Jesus came to set the oppressed free, He now passed the task to us when He made the great commission, He said it all. We are to implement the rule of the love of God, let us pass that on to the people, we all know that the rule of God is love for us all. To love the oppressed is to fear God because His eye is on them. Jesus proclaimed good news to the poor by saying that the kingdom has come, and his recovery for sight to the blind is like this, spiritually we are blind, there is no point in telling people that we can see when His truth is not revealed to us, spiritually we are blind. (Exodus 34:6) (NIV) God's core character traits are rooted in generous mercy and loyal love, God is not happy to see us suffering but to see us happy and prospering, look at what He did when the devil had decided to oppress us for ever, He gave His only begotten Son that we should not perish but to have everlasting life. I know we are trying to emulate Him and we also try to live but our love comes nowhere near His love because our love is selective. If we want to do like Him, we have to ask Him to help us because on our own we may fail to get to that type of love because His is unconditional. Sometimes we tend to think that this life is all what we have and forget that there is eternal life to be live so we have to prepare for that eternal life yet we have to start practising it here on earth. Eternal life is a life of loving one another, to sum the whole story up is to say God is love. Whatever God does, He plans in time so for the coming of Jesus as the Messiah was well planned. When Isaiah gave a prophecy for the coming of Jesus, His whole mission on earth was for the oppressed, whoever is oppressing people is against the mission of Christ. We are under God's favour to be able to read and understand for ourselves and to be able to get someone who can explain scripture to us so that we know the requirements of the Lord. We have to get prepared for the day, this day is still coming when there will be judgement. We have to be informed that He is using mercy, so we are living in the times of His favour. (Luke 4:18) (NIV) This verse got people mixed up in their minds, because when He said that He had come to set the people free they thought of being freed from the captivity in Babylon, buy yet they were still under the rule of the Roman Empire, that is where He was misunderstood, yet God works His plan and not man's plan, so when Jesus said this scripture has been fulfilled today in your eyes, they became more confused and started accusing Him of blasphemy that they sought to kill Him. (Isaiah 61:1-3) (NIV) Jesus is always just, He wants justice for everyone, in His eyes He sees equality for everyone. When one is oppressed, that person will suffer psychologically, which may result in one getting depressed, oppression is the unjust use of power at other people's expense. This is found mostly in those with power, you have to be careful how you use this power because you may end up using it to oppress other people.

Think of power in a broad sense, it could be a government official, church members, company managers going down to individuals, how do we look at those below us or how do you look at those below you? Are you treating them as equals? The way you are treating them, would you like to be treated like that, if not, then it is time to change and start on a clean page today. This happens when you forget that those you are oppressing do not belong to you, but to their creator. Oppression is around us all the time. What one should do in order to avoid doing it yourself on others, you have to think that how would you feel if it were you, always put yourself in their shoes. You should always think of Christianity if you want to stop oppressing other people because Christ is the creator of them. The good order of living is to treat all human beings equally, once you start thinking in the lines of equality, you will not oppress others. If you are in a position of power, you must always guard against misusing that power. The powerful take more for themselves at the expense of the weaker ones. This can be done through violent means, if the individual is stronger than the other it could be on the level of nations if the other might have a stronger army than the other, it may result in them taking what they want and leave what is not wanted to the weaker. This is not fair in the eyes of God, something He does not expect from people who claim to be His people.

If you claim to be a child of God, then treat others as equals. How are you treating those who are inferior too you? If I am an agent of enforcing the law, am I enforcing it accordingly? Or I may overdo it taking advantage of being in that position. Please treat anyone under you equally, for they are created the same as you, for the same measure you are using today is the same measure that will be used to you.

The was scripture is inspired by God, so, to understand it we must ask for His Holy Spirit to guide and to make us understand what is in it. The reason why He put them in the scriptures, He wants us to understand them so that we can build relationship with Him. The reason why we should ask for divine revelation in order to understand the differences between the two is that the kingdom of Heaven is invisible while the Earthly kingdom is visible. The heavenly kingdom is invisible, that is why we should always ask for divine revelation so as to be able to understand and to be able to do things that will enable you to be accommodated into this kingdom.

13

We Believe that the Kingdom has Already Come

I t is for us to ask for a revelation to be able to see that the kingdom of God is among us, if we can be able to note that the kingdom is already among us, so that means we have faith. We are encouraged to know that the kingdom has already come, God has already fulfilled His purpose. We have to ask for an understanding that if the coming of Jesus meant that the kingdom has already come then we have to ask for an understanding that since He said He would be with us in spirit He is present in us today His church is functioning through His Spirit. What we have to ask God is to make us to be able to accept that kingdom, because the kingdom cold be here, but without the understanding that it is here, we go on and on without knowing it. The kingdom of God comes through us after repentance and staying a pure life of following Jesus' footsteps. During the time of Jesus, there was a very religious group called the pharisees, as these people thought they were perfect, they missed the point forgetting that our flesh could be tempted and the world could be so attractive that we might be led astray, the devil uses our flesh and the world. We must ask God to redeem us so that we can be able to resist those temptations. As God put His Holy Spirit in us, He expects us to advance His kingdom on earth. Sometimes we go against God because we want Him to act according to our plan and not according to His plan, let us fall into His plan.

When Jesus said the kingdom has come, He expected us to respond and repent in order to qualify for the kingdom of heaven that has come for it requires repentance and we will be transformed, because the heavenly kingdom requires pure people. The kingdom itself is a pure kingdom inhabited by righteous people. It is sad to note that, although it was preached over and over in the Old Testament, people expected the Messiah to come in a very surprising way. This was not the way with Jesus, hence so many people missed the target. Are we not going in the same way? Are we not mixing with Jesus without taking any note of it?

Let us be vigilant and know that there is no difference between them and us. Everything is now put to us in writing. It is now for us to ask for divine revelation, in order for us to see Christ in whatever we do. Let God's Spirit work in people, if that happens then we start seeing that the kingdom has already come.

The Kingdom of Heaven Brings Happiness

If the coming of Jesus is good news, and Jesus brought the heavenly kingdom, then there is happiness in the heavenly kingdom. What the heavenly kingdom requires of us to enjoy this happiness is to repent. When you repent that means you are born again, to be born again is to leave your old ways of doing things and do things the way the Lord requires. To live in Christ means to have your life overhauled and surrender ourselves to the one who will look after our souls. To live the life of the kingdom is to live a life led by the Holy Spirit, which if you are living a life led by the Holy Spirit you are living in the trinity. To be led by the Holy Spirit, it will make you fear the Lord yet fear the Lord will make you live in happiness. By accepting God, you are making Him ruler of your soul and heart, if He lives in your heart, that means He will manifest to the world through you. To repent is to do our part of the process, and the Lord His part that means you will be living a life blessed by the Lord. If you are doing what the Lord commands, that means you love Him with all your mind and with all your soul, loving the Lord like that it means it is the source of happiness. Spend most of your time with the lord, that means the devil has no time to be with you, so it is you who will choose who to be with, it is not just a coincident who to be with, but it is you who chooses your life style not someone else. When God answers your prayers, you must be ready to accept His answers, by the way you respond to Him you will make Him delighted in you. God call us to holiness not to happiness, He wants us to honour Him by our daily choices and overall lifestyle. The Bible tells us there is right and wrong God loves us when we do the right thing. There are some things we do which make us but do the Lord no good He does not like us to do things that do not please Him. When you repent do not go to the old way of doing things but to live according to what the Lord requires us to live. If you are always trusting in the Lord and taking a delight in all His deeds it means He will give you all the desires of your heat.

What is God's Spirit Doing to People's Hearts?

It is very unwise to try to hide our deeds, yet God sees what is in our hearts. Once we know that He sees what is in our hearts, we can be able to confess our sins and He is faithful enough to cleanse us, so that we can be as white as snow. We should always ask God to lead us into the life of walking in the spirit than walking in the flesh. To walk by the spirit means to be always doing the will of God, which means we will not be doing as the flesh pleases, but as the Lord pleases, rules, or the moral conduct us to walk the Spiritual life. How do I walk in the spirit? To walk in the spirit, means to always strive to do exactly as Christ was doing or to always do as the Lord pleases, that means it is not the lust of the flesh, but as the Lord pleases. (Galatians 5:16) (NIV) What we always should strive for, is to invite the Lord to dwell in us so that whatever we do will always be led by the spirit. "For the flesh lusts against the spirit, and spirit against the flesh, and these are contrary one to the other, so you cannot do the things that you would. But if you are led by the Spirit, you are not under the law." If you obey the Spirit, that means you are above the law. The Holy Spirit has to lead us to love without being compelled by the law, joy which comes on its own, if you walk in the Spirit, the Lord will always give you joy, you will lead a life of joy all your life. Sometimes we make ourselves believe that we have peace when it is not lasting peace yet peace that is everlasting comes from the Lord. Peace not that you disobey the law, but that you are always ahead of what the law would ask you to do, you have already done it before it asks you to do it, that is doing what is good. That comes from the Lord, this gives you gentleness in life and also to have faith in the Lord which means you have a closer relationship with Him always. If you do that, the love of Christ will always be in your actions all your life. The life of honouring the Lord will always produce good fruits because you will always have fervent love for peace. Paul was concerned with what was happening to the Galatians people. The reason why Paul was concerned with the Galatian people was that they were confused whether to follow the law of Moses or to follow Christ? They were always disputing each other, which was a sign that they were living in the flesh, living in the flesh means that you are always rebellious against the law of God and do what pleases your flesh. This means that you are always contrary to Spiritual things and doing what pleases your flesh, so Paul was pleading with them to live in spirit, so as to have the fruits of the spirit. Paul knew that they were missing the Holiness of God which makes our sad life to live without the Lord (Romans 8:5-6) (NIV).

14

God and Mankind

Holy Scriptures Show why God Created Mankind

Humans would like to know why mankind was created, and what life means. We are all called by the name of God, God created us for His glory, meaning that we have to give glory to Him always He deserves that when God created a man, this He did for a man to give all the praise and revere Him. Our business as Christians is to tell the world what God has done to us, and who He is, (Isaiah 43:7) (NIV). When God said "Let us make man in our image," He used the plural, it is correct both ways, to say that they, the trinity, and to say plural is used for kings whether He is one, it's they. To be made in the image of God is not in flesh or in physical form, but in Spirit. A man is greatly honoured to be made in the image of God, and all His likeness and on top of being made in the likeness of God, man was given dominion over everything on earth. Man was given a very big responsibility, we were made to stand for the kingdom of heaven, whatever we do or whatever we say must be for the heavenly kingdom. To be fruitful as He said, we should always do good because we are representing the heavenly kingdom, (Genesis 1:26) (NIV). We may want to represent the kingdom as much as we may want to, but with the forces of darkness, we may not be able to achieve our goal, but with His help, we may be able to, (Ephesians 3:9-10) (NIV) Unbelievers think that when something bad happens to Christians, the Lord is not there, no these things happen to everyone but now it depends on how we receive it, God will always be on our side to make us overcome them, (Colossians 1:16) (NIV).

God Created us for His Glory

It is fitting that man must give glory to God because man was made in God's image and put His Spirit in Him. At creation, we hear that He spoke ad it was done, but on man we hear that He formed and made. (Genesis 1:26-27) (NIV) Then God said, 'Let us make man in Our image, according to Our likeness, So God created man in his own image; in the image of God, He created male and female He created them. It is a statement of intent, unlike others which were statements of action. An example of a statement of action is verse 3: Then God said, 'Let there be light; and there was light. This qualifies the statement that "God created us for His glory:

Jesus Christ was conceived of the Spirit; He became flesh like us. As if that was not enough on creation, after he had led man astray into the bondage of sin, and was to be held in the devil's captivity for ever, Jesus came and ransomed us and redeemed us for ever, one good turn deserves another, so man must give all the glory to God.

Who is the Least in the Kingdom of God?

(Matthew 5:19) (NIV) Jesus wants to make it clear to us that there are sins we might take as small issues or small sins, Jesus wants you to take note of those small sins and let yourself stay pure in the eyes of God. Jesus gave examples as being angry, we might think that we are not committing a sin by being angry, but that is a sin. You may not commit adultery but you committing a sin by lusting. If you want to be great in the kingdom of God you have to observe those small sins you would expect to be the least but will make you to be the least in the kingdom of God

So do not just ignore those you think are of little effect they will affect your eternal life, this is the time to work for eternal life. Encourage others to also observe and to take them seriously if you want to be great in the kingdom of God. So according to this, it will mean there will be different status in heaven according to this saying. This teaches us that what we teach people to do, is the way we have done it ourselves or what we instruct others to do we have done it ourselves. Do not instruct anyone to do bad, to steal, or kill for you will be answerable for that according to the teaching of Jesus in this scripture.

15

The Ten
Commandments –
Nailed to the Cross

uke 1:6) (NIV)The ten commandments and the ordinances are not the same thing and are separate. Ordinances generally govern matters that are not covered by state or federal laws examples of ordinances would be, those related to noise snow removal, pet restrictions and building and zoning regulations. examples are: authoritative decree or direction. Law set forth by a governmental authority specifically municipal regulation A city ordinance forbids construction work to start before 8 am an ordinance is equivalent of statute, passed by a city council, county council or equivalent body.

(Hebrews 9:1-2) (NIV) (Colossians 2:14-17) (NIV) having cancelled the charge of our legal indebtedness which stood against us, and condemned us; He has taken it away, nailed it to the cross. We have to examine our lives and most of all, we should transform our lives modelling them to Jesus' life.

The Bible Reveals Your Future and Purpose for Existing

The purpose of existence is to live together in harmony, when we live in harmony, we make life easy for one another. God fulfils His purpose for you, when you disobey God's laws you are not living in God's purpose. It is you who is distancing yourself from Him, not Him forsaking you, so it is better for you to speak to Him who will fulfil His purpose to you. Do your part and He will do His part? God's plan to us is not to make us miserable or make us poor or desperate, what He wants to see on us is to see us prosper in our lives. Before we were born, God prepared our destiny, what He wants to see is that we have accomplished our destiny. Jesus set an example of obedience although that obedience led Him to suffer. We have to be obedient even it seems difficult, it pays in the end. For this, we have to turn to the Bible for the revelation of our destiny, to get this revelation, we have to pray to be able to understand the meaning hidden in it. Always the Bible reveals what God wants us to do, and what He promised He would do to us. If we obey Him, we will live a divine life, well guided We will meet the future well guided by God. We are all working for eternal life, we have to start practicing for that life by loving one another, God is happy to see us love one another. For our future, we have to keep on praying to Him in order to reveal the future for us. We should stay in prayer, although God planned our lives before, we still have to pray in order to keep connected, below and above. Reading His word keeps us also close to Him because those scriptures were inspired by Him, they are our lives' guidance. Let us ask Him to keep our hearts as pure as we can because this is where He makes a relationship with us. Let us pray that He makes our community a godly community, who always says "holy, holy, holy" because if we stay in that environment, that will help us also to stay Godly. We pray to Him to make us to love the truth because if we love to be truthful that will mean that everything we do if we do it honestly, this pleases God.

The main Purpose a Man was Created

A man has to achieve his purpose willingly, a man has to comprehend the world around him, since a man is here to represent the heavenly kingdom. A man has to bear in mind that he is a steward of God looking after all God's creations. Man must strive to fulfil the purpose because he was created in the image of God. The problem that a man faces is of greediness, a man is never contented with what he has, yet to be contended is not to say we stop working. Sometimes, this greediness is caused by wanting glory for ourselves. We have to realise that we have a short period in this life, the purpose of which is to work for the Lord, as His expectations of making us in His own image.

16

Trinity

How do I Join God's Family, the Trinity?

Have you ever noticed how you have tried to distance yourself from God, but He still cares for you? That shows how much love He has for us, and how he cares for us. It does not matter how far you had gone when you come back, He forgives you and welcomes you back into the fold. Jesus said, I came that they may have life and have it abundantly" (John 10:10) (NIV). At one time or another, we have sinned against the Lord knowingly or not knowingly, and that has distanced us from the Lord, and we know very well that the result of sin is death, (Romans 6:23) (NIV) It is us who would have died where Jesus died in our stead, to die for someone's sin means true love, something we must emulate, (1 Corinthians 15:3-4) (NIV) Since we have been saying that we are sinning against Him time and again, so we have to repent to be saved, we are saved by His grace alone. God sent His Son on earth in order for us to get to know Him better. Now we know we have to love Him better than before, we were told that for the holy spirit to live in us we have to stay pure, this means that, if the holy spirit stays in us, and Him being a member of the trinity, that means we are also members of the Trinity, which is a perfect Family. Their love of man is the one that made them say "Let us make man in our image", it was through love. If we are going astray, we have to remember that as we love our children, we copied it from our father who loves us dearly. We love the Trinity because it loves us and our lives reflect the trinity. The Holy Spirit makes us to be in the trinity. The Pentecostals reject the Trinity as pagan.

Because of love, God does not abandon His creation, He upholds and sustains His creation. The Holy Spirit breathes life into our nostrils and sets us free from sin, He is the source of creation, divine love, and is the source of redemption, love, and uniting us to God. The Trinitarian relationship is connection between the Father, Son, and the Holy Spirit. The Holy Spirit is the presence of God in the world, often represented as a dove, the Trinity helps Christians to have a deeper understanding of God and how He can be all the things the Bible suggests. The Holy Spirit enters the plan of salvation through His personal action at Jesus' life making Him Son of God in humanity. This is the Comforter sent by Christ at the end of His mission on earth. The view of the Mammon differs from that of Christianity. Christians believe in the Trinity, believing that we are saved through faith in Christ alone and not with our works. We have to realise that before we could do any works, God loved man and gave Hi Son to die for our sins, in return to such love we have to have faith that Jesus died for us.

To be a Christian Means to be like Christ

The problem with Christianity is that many profess to be Christians without following exactly what is required to be a Christian. Yet the real meaning is to say like Christ, means we have to follow His footsteps, which we all know what He went through. There are so many things which lead us not to comply because of mare deceit, some because of confusion some because of falsehood, His name should be unique, no any other name where people should get any salvation than under His name. The only way to be in a good relationship with Him is to accept Him into your heart. To become a Christian, we have to follow God's example, as He loved us, He gave us His only Son, so Christianity is all about love. If we follow Christ and try to do as He did in every step if we do that with all our hearts, there is no way He might say He does not know you, let us remember that we are not saved by our works but by faith. Since we inherited this sin from the first creation, all have sinned and came short for the glory of God.

The Truth About Christianity

We have to be obedient to all God' commandments for they are meant to build relationship between us and God. The word Christianity has become so used that we now tend to say it without thinking or without deepening our thoughts. The way Christ came to this earth is what makes us start asking, because we may not have a revelation yet, let us ask for it to be revealed to us like it was done to Peter that Jesus said to him it is not flesh and blood that has revealed this to you but my Father in heaven. Without anything to prove that He was the Messiah, He grew up like an ordinary child, we all know what is to be like an ordinary child, who would believe that at thirty He would start to claim that He was the Messiah. That is why He even said, a prophet has no glory in his home country. The fact that He grew up with them blinded them that even though He performed those miracles that could not convince them.

We as people who are studying scriptures, we should not be taken unawares like what was happening to those who had not studied scriptures. It is good for us because we are also being guided by the Holy Spirit who can reveal the meaning. I think we are undergoing a phase in our lives that one day we will have to reflect. It may appear in the eyes of people as if Christianity was fading, but the truth is that God will remain on His throne, it is required to be implanted in people's minds that it is us who are changing and not Him changing. What one has to bear in mind is that there is a battle raging falsehood and the truth between faith and unbelief, so the war is not over yet. It appears there is a heavy storm raging but it will still come to pass and the sea will be calm again. My plea to my fellow Christians is, let us hold on to our faith this shall come to pass. All this tide is there to those who will have survived that tide to be able to reflect and be able to recall how they rode through the tide; they will be sharing on how they managed when it was so tempting that many fell by the wayside. But as Christians it is not for us to be reflecting on that but to be telling the story of, we managed to carry them along with us during those trying times.

The Lord desires that we understand him because He ways of doing things is quite different from ours. Sometimes it was said things were going to change for the better, although it was expected for things to change for the better, things did not change. Things got even worse and still are, the Lord we believe in does His things for a purpose of which we are not His advisers to tell Him where to drive His ship. Our prayers to Him are, Lord remember us. There is a saying that a fish rots from the head is what we are witnessing today that where Christianity was spreading all over the world from is where it is declining from, intelligence appears to have victory over the world of religion.

(Exodus 20:1-17) (NIV) It appears we are now doing the contrary, God said you shall have no other gods before me. We are doing the opposite Sometimes we take things the other way round because if we take the ten commandments the other way, they will be a burden, yet they were meant to God's people all the Holiness they were meant to be. What went wrong was that they were misinterpreted thinking that if we obey God's laws, we are going to be prosperous, God is not going to let any nations invade us, this might also be happening today that we are having the wrong concept of what it means to obey God's laws. I pray that we stay guided into the correctness of it so that we do not go astray.

(Matthew 22:37-39) (NIV) God is love, so if we love God and love our neighbour, we are following His footsteps. If we follow his footsteps means we will be like Him if He is love that will mean we are doing true Christianity. Let us do all what we can to show our love to Him as He loved us.

17

What is the True Conversion?

omans 8:9) (NIV) Conversion means to be transformed to completely leave your old state and become a new creation. This means to be controlled by the Holy Spirit, you are no longer controlled by the flesh, when you realise that you have been serving idols, you reject your old way of doing things, turn away completely and follow ways of God and start living a Godly life. Always studying the word of God and change the way you live and completely to be always committed to the word of God, will strengthen your faith in Him. To be honest when dealing with people, truthfulness in your daily life. An upright life and ready to suffer for the Lord, and helping to fight evil in the community. Your daily living must show that you are a changed creation you are God's vessel. There is a difference between conversion and repentance, conversion means you are completely turned from an old being to a new being.

True conversion is the fruit of faith, repentance, and consistence obedience, when you hear the word of God and keep it that means you are being faithful to the word, with the help of the Holy Spirit we will try to keep what we hear from the word. When you confess that means you have left your old ideas you become a new creation. Conversion means a lot, because it means making God the centre of our lives If He is the centre of our lives that we will be loving the world as He did.

Becoming a new Creation in God

To say that you are a new creation in God means that your ways of doing things have completely changed, the way you are doing things now pleases God. (2 Corinthians 5:17) (NIV), to receive Christ is to be created anew, in Christ means all the old things are gone and everything is new and even you are also a new creation. To be called to Christ is to be called to put on your new self, by implementing the teachings of Jesus we will be like Him, so the first thing is to invite Him into our lives. When you have faith in Christ and He accepts you that means He will make you a new creation who is acceptable into His kingdom. We all love new things, so that is what Christ does if we are new creations, He loves us. God is Spirit, if we love Him and He accepts us that means we are living in spirit because we emulating spiritual things. That means we have stopped looking at Christ as human being but as a spiritual so that will mean that we are in spirit. When we are emulating Him and being like Him who is Spirit. When you love Christ and He loves you, we all lived in the past where we did not know who Jesus was but He was kind enough to carry us along like that until such time we were able to see new things and we had time to make up our minds. Because of His kindness He taught us the new covenant and that the old had passed away (John 1:13) (NIV) By old and new, it means that we had our old way of doing things, and since Jesus has taught us new way of doing things and we have taken the new way of doing things we must be new creations. When we come to realise that our old ways of doing things were bad, we must abandon those old ways and get new ways of doing things and become new creation. If we continue to sin that means we are living in the past, let us ask God that when we leave the old ways, help us not to go back to the old, let us ask the Lord to sanctify us daily so that we stay his children.

The True Gospel?

When Jesus came to this world He brought good news, this means when we follow it, it will lead us to salvation. The truth is that, when God decided to give us His only begotten Son, we had not asked Him for that, we are all sinners who were condemned to death but He was kind enough to redeem us so that we can be assured of heaven. The good news that God loves sinners, since the first man sinned, we were all born sinners and condemned to death. Jesus came to look for us and now we are fit for heaven through His blood. Being fit for heaven is not automatic, you are on the receiving end, you have to realise that you are a sinner and repent from your sins. Without repentance, you cannot be saved, the punishment of sin is the second death (Colossians 1:14) The gospel came specially to rescue us from the forces of darkness in which were put in by the lies of the devil. Since the gospel came to rescue us, the one who believes in it will see the light. (Romans 10: 9) (NIV), to get salvation, you have to say it with your own mouth, it is for you to receive the Lord for the Lord has been taught to us that there is no salvation in any other than in Christ Jesus. (John 3;16) (NIV) God's love is unconditional so when we are asked to love Him it is not a condition but to say, if someone loves you it will be automatic that you love back that person not that you are told to love but that it is a reciprocal. You just feel like you want to return the love. This being saved is not automatic, we have to believe that Christ died on the cross for us, repent and walk in His ways and never to go back to the old ways of doing things, hold firm to the way the Bible teaches you. Do not let the devil take away what you already have, as it was preached to you and you accepted. The laws of God are not as corrupt as the laws of this corrupt world. These laws are meant to strengthen our relationship with God. He is Holy, how can we be related to Him if we are not Holy? If we are like Him, then we become members of the heavenly family whose business is to praise and give glory to God Day and night, (yet there is no night there.)

18

Christianity and Slavery

How do Christians Justify Being Slave Owners?

There is some significance in the year 1619 that is, some 400 years ago, in America in the state of Virginia slaves were traded for some supplies. This is the time when the American people in all the different states agreed to create a single government that would represent all the 49 states, (they would call this a Representative Government for all the forty-nine states). This was the time when they recorded the twenty first slaves who arrived in Virginia America were recorded, this was in 1619, before that, there were some Africans who were enslaved in America in the 1500s, but they were not yet keeping accurate records. Portuguese were leading in selling these people from Angola as slaves to America. This evil act of buying of people as slaves, known as (slave trade) went on for over two centuries.

The Lord works in a mysterious way, who knew that this could be abolished by now. Jesus once said, "it is not for you to know what my Father has set in His kingdom," we have to be still and know that He is God, when slavery was abolished, some have resorted to hidden slavery which we are witnessing to this day, He is still working on it that one day it may be completely abolished. During this period, people who were sold as slaves were about 12.5 million captives, they did not approve what they were involved in because it was unfavourable to them they were taken from Africa across the Atlantic, known as the, Some years later Ghana and Senegal joined Angola was ruled by the Portuguese then, who were involved in selling people as captive to America. Only Ninja Mbande the queen of the Ndonga and Mataba kingdoms did not approve this trade of people refused to sell her people. Sometimes our Christianity is questionable, Christians to be doing things that a non-Christian did not do, this will not go well with Christianity, if you look at things like this. The writer is really concerned with this being carried out by people who claimed to be Christians, this means if this is the case Christianity has to be revisited. Even the clergy enslaved people, there were slaves who were owned by missionary Organisations that belonged to the Anglican churches in the United States of America. These people lost their identity, they were sent in large groups to America, this was another factor which made them lose their their identity disappeared as they were destroyed. Overall, slaves were treated unfairly, with the exception of a very few minorities depending on if a slave owner was born good at heart but such good owners could only be a very small percentage, about 10%. This harsh treatment made some slaves to think of risking escaping, but according to the laws those days, if they were caught the punishment, would be death. They would use the Bible without asking for guidance from the Lord. They would use the Bible to justify their misdeeds and still claim to be true Christians. There is a good reason when we say we have to ask for a revelation. In order We should ask Him to lead us to interpret the Bible, because it is the same Bible used by slave owners to justify themselves. They were treating these slaves harshly, but they claimed that they were treating them legally, and fairly.

If the same Bible that was used by slave owners is the same bible used by slaves, then we must ask for a revelation in order to strike a compromise. On one hand slave masters used the to justify enslaving fellow human beings, then on the other hand, the slaves used the same Bible to cry to the Lord so that He could hear what they were going through and asking Him to hear their prayers.

Twenty slaves arrived in Virginia in 1619, they were the first to arrive in America at the port of that state, but this was against their will. Those who do not claim to be Christians are not classified here, but Christians cannot justify themselves here. In a group of people, it becomes difficult when some people have a revelation and others have not. In their churches, there were often some disagreements because of some mixed feelings about human life: a Christian should value human life. If there is no such feeling, then we have to revise our life application.

On the other hand, there were primitive or cruel Africans, who, when they were wronged, would sell their kinsman. That is why this slave trade flourished.

It is better to remember that even today temptations are still there and they will be there. It is not advisable to try to put the blame on God or to try to justify our wrongdoings, other than repenting and ask to be forgiven and to ask to be Spirit-filled, we cannot escape the reality by trying to justify ourselves. The Bible can still be used to try to justify oppressing the children of God, it all depends on how it is interpreted. During the Atlantic Slave trade, the Bible was used by Christians on both sides of the issue, and the abolitionists who sought to bring it to an end. Slave trade was established for economic reasons, because that meant that the slave owners would get free labour, meaning that whatever they got from the sale of their products was all profit because they did not pay for the labour. The abolition of slave trade would mean unprofitable to those who sold slaves, and those who had plantations, it meant unprofitable to those who owned plantations because it meant they were no more getting that free labour. Things follow one another, in the modern day, things have taken different turn, it is being tactfully done, because instead of making it a free labour, they are now maximising their profits for a very small wadge they are giving to their workers, which has turned to slavery with a sugar coating.

People are created differently, there are some who want to make profit at any cost, this means they do not care whether it means making profit on someone's blood. There are some who believe that a person was created in the image of God so there should be no making of profit on someone's blood, so, when they were fighting for the abolition of slave trade, they were fighting for a moral reason. Even to this day if your way of making money is evil, you can still find some other ways of making money through clean means. There was debate that went on until congress passed a law on January 31 of the year 1865, ratified on December 6 1865, 13th amendment abolished slavery in the United States of America provides that neither slavery nor involuntary servitude, except on punishment for crimes where any one is duly convicted, shall exist throughout the United States of America.) On the first day of the first month of the year 1863 Abraham Lincoln signed into law, what was agreed on the abolition of slave trade which made America as it is today.

The Bible and Slavery

Those who were proslavery and those who wanted it abolished, all were quoting from that same Bible, that means there is still a lot to be learned about the interpretation of the bible, since we have all different interpretations, are they all right? Paul has always been advising slave owners to treat their slaves as human beings, and has been reminding them that they also have a master in heaven.

The reason why there are so many churches today is that everyone tends to interpret the Bible in their own way that suits them, so the time of slavery was no exception. So, it is quite clear now that it is not enough to just quote the Bible without asking for a revelation. For example, Paul did not say abolish slavery, but what did he mean when he said, treat slaves as brothers, he meant that there should be no slavery.

As Christians, when looking at slavery, we should look at it from both angles: those who bought slaves found a ready market from Africa. Why? When we look at it, we must look at it in the way that will make us see on the justice side and see justice to the whole case. When we look at things, we must also look at the root cause of it. Did those people in Africa value human life? They should not have sold their kinsmen in the first place. It appears, even to this day, African governments appear not to value human life much. Lives are being lost in seas, people running away from African rule, and choosing to go for voluntary slavery in some first world countries. African governments do not care whether people are dying in seas running away from their rule, as long as they are ruling.

The (Bicentenary) 200 years of the Abolition of Slave Trade

What is most surprising today is why there is vast difference today with the spirit that sprang up in those days to end slave trade. It appears like that spirit is still there but we are ignoring it, choosing to stay without asking for us to be clothed. There was shown a spirit of togetherness, but today you can hardly see that spirit. Although governments have put laws that say there should be no separation you will notice that spirit is being practised in churches with no sign of it being discouraged. As we celebrate two hundred years there has to be rethink of this because it appears worse now than it was before wondering what really has gone wrong. The gospel is being preached, but to what extend or how far is it convicting those who are preaching it, or it is just taken as a duty.

Whichever way we might try to preach the gospel it still remains with a question mark to whoever is preaching it. Modern day slavery has shown no sign of going away too soon than it is showing that it is going to be there for a fore see able future. This has got to be looked into, if it is not looked into sooner than later, it appears the gap is widening. The church should not be silent knowing what damage was made to Christianity, knowing that the churches took part in such deeds. Let us re new our Christianity, because Christianity should not have those dark sports. We tend to think that as time goes on it will die a natural death, not taking into consideration that there are some dark forces fighting Christianity. We need to be in one accord in order to fight this kind of darkness. It has to be bone in mind that scriptures were used to enslave people, we might be trading the same way but in the most modern way of Biblical interpretation which takes us nowhere

Slavery has left its mark on Christianity, that mark is visible and is there for everyone to see and to act on it. The author is appealing to every Christian to say let us do something other than leaving it to the next generation. How do we expect society to deal with that problem, the church has to make a start and society will follow suite. Let us not wait for those who did it during the times of William Wilberforce to come and do it again for us today.

On Christianity, this fight of modern-day slavery should not be left to one side of Christianity let us look at it holistically. It is very easy for Christians to be carried away, instead of fighting for the survival of Christianity it appears most will be seeking wealth in a very mild way, but most have drifted into wealth. It appears the devil has found a way of carrying them away without them realising it, by the time they will realise, they will have drifted very far from the original, and makes it difficult to find their way back. If Christianity came to Africa during the second half of the second century, but to this day Africans are still streaming to those first world countries to seek theological studies which might find us grappling our way to try to find out what is happening. Whatever reason might be given, it has shown that there is still a long way to go in trying to study what is causing all this. No matter what defence might be given the fact still remains that something has to be rectified which needs oneness and a lot of consultation. Whichever way one might answer it, there is still need for a study to be made in order to come up with a clear picture and to try to find a solution.

It appears when the stories such as the one brought by some people who were antislavery are not perused but left to gather dust and they die a natural death. What is required today is to study the history of slave trade and especially its effect on human dignity and not to leave it as history. We have to bear in mind that it has not remained in history, but that it has changed tactic and has become modern day slavery and has got to find a modern-day solution which should not be left to individual grouping but to be dealt with holistically if we want to find a solution for this, we have to play our part as individuals as groups as organisations we must see the task in front of us as everyone's problem which requires everyone's solution.

The author is appealing to all like, churches, government organisations such as clubs, voluntary organisation, groups and individuals this is everyone's problem which requires everyone's solution or every individual's effort. Whichever way you might want to look at it we have to come together for a solution.

They were giving excuses that they were taking Africans to America in order them to become Christians. But even today Africans are still going to America to study Christianity, is this by coincidence or is it by some making of some powers behind it? This is food for thought.

The Rule in Africa

It can still be seen today that there are some people who are running away from their country to seek refuge in those countries who were accused of treating slaves badly. They are running away from fellow Africans, going to seek voluntary slavery in foreign countries again which are still making them slaves, this slavery has now got a sugar coating. To swallow a bitter pill, you must put a sugar coating on it, that is the slavery which is being experienced these days with no light seen at the end of the tunnel, it appears this is going to continue for some time. the way the African rulers are ruling in some form of dictating calling it democracy. The plea to both sides is to treat human life with all the respect that it deserves, otherwise the future still looks bleak. Before we start to value life as someone who was created in the image of God. This means whenever you see a human being you have seen the image of God. Without the respect for human life, we may still be going generation after generation without a solution yet. The title of this book is: Contrast between the earthly kingdom and the heavenly kingdom. This shows, there is a difference in these kingdoms. There is no point in asking the Lord Day and night that your kingdom come without us being transformed. We must be asking the Lord to transform us so that the heavenly kingdom must be manifested in us. Those small things we think do not matter are the things which are preventing us from seeing the kingdom of God. It is us who must strive to make that kingdom to come. Asking the Lord for His kingdom to come must be a formality of something we are practising. So, it has to be all sided, meaning that we must be praying and practising it, so how they are ruling in heaven will be how this world will be ruled.

There are some people or organisations which campaigned strongly that all people should be equal in the eyes of God. Everyone should receive the light of God regardless of where they come from. If physical or spiritual slavery is a consequence of sinful action, what sinful action did those the Atlantic Slave Trade commit before? Normally when something bad befalls you, it is often associated with darkness, although it does not necessarily mean it follows one another. Those slave owners who did not allow their slaves to go to church means that they knew that what they were doing was wrong. In other cases, some slave owners did not allow their slaves to go to church, because they feared that if they know the Bible they would start rebelling against slavery, so some of them for not knowing the scriptures were not a fault of their own. So, these slave owners know that they are doing something wrong that is why they did not want the people's eyes opened. This has been put in present tense, because it is still happening in people's minds to this day.

So, if those slave masters did not like their slaves to go to church, just because if they knew the Bible, they would revolt against slavery, that means they knew that they were doing something wrong. It is only that they did not want to admit that what they were doing was wrong.

History clearly states that Christianity started in Africa in the middle of the first century, that by the beginning of the 2nd century it had already spread from Egypt to Ethiopia.

Slaves were Shipped Across the Atlantic: The Bible was used to Justify

But if we ask for the revelation and to ask to be guided by the Holy Spirit, we would not interpret it the way we want because it is inspired by God. It appears the Bible can always be interpreted the way that suits the interpreter. The Christians of those days were both sides proslavery Christians and Slavery Abolitionists were all basing on the Bible. Christians need to ask for a revelation to be able to interpret according to what the scripture really means. For example, Paul seems to have not condemned Slavery, but when he sent Onesimus back to Philemon, he said do not take him as a slave anymore but take him as a brother, which means in Christ we are brothers, not slave and master. Yes, we may say slave trade was abolished, but how much of this is still being practiced today undercover? Are we taking or treating each other with brotherly love, meaning that we are sons and daughters of the same Father? This shows clearly how the earthly kingdom is different from the heavenly kingdom.

History shows that Christianity played a part in enslaving people, they used the Bible in all this, such as (Genesis 9:24-27) (NIV). If a person is cursed by the Lord, who are we to intervene in that cursing as well? People were very much attracted to wealth to such an extent that they compromise their Christianity. As a church today, how are we accumulating our wealth? Some of the ways we may use to accumulate wealth may be against humanity. Such were the ways used by slave owners to acquire wealth by being cruel to humanity, claiming to be paying tithes with ill-gotten money. The mission of the church is to bring all souls to Christ, regardless of whether that soul is Gentile or Jew. These days it is appearing that as long as a person who suffers the ill-treatment is of a different race, it appears to go well with us, we just say let us carry on as if things were normal. It appears individuals are leaving it to the church, while the church is leaving it to the government and vice-versa. The case of humanity has to be treated with urgency. This must start with us individuals, without leaving it to the church or government, the ball is in our court as individuals to have a conviction in our inner feelings, let it start from there, and let it manifest from us.

Christianity reached Egypt in the middle of the first century AD. At the end of the 2nd century AD, it had spread as far as Ethiopia and Eritrea. It contrasts what was said by pro-slavery Christians that it was good for the Africans to have been brought to America as slaves, they would learn Christianity, yet it was there in Africa already. If they were being taken to America to learn Christianity, why then were they taken there as slaves?

Conflicting Statements on Slavery

How did slavery originate, and what are the factors that that contribute to its start? Scholars seem not to agree on the origin of slavery, because they say, as most slaves were from Africa, therefore, they were the descendance of Canaan the son of Ham the cursed son of Noah.

Some scholars say, Biblically, Canaanites are identified in Genesis as descendance of Canaan son of Ham and grandson of Noah. DNA evidence shows that human genetic, shows that the Canaanites did not just disappear. Instead, they survived and are the ancestors of the people now living in modern day Lebanon.

During the time of slave trade there was always some debate between proslavery Christians and some abolitionists. The abolitionists appear to have won, but it appears the battle has not yet been won because they have changed the tactic. It is now done in such a way that it cannot be noticed, people are now given a wage that is not proportional to the work done, or to the profit that is made by the organisation. Like before, it was not everyone who owned slaves, the same thing still applies, it may not be all organisations but some are doing it. The reason why people owned slaves is that they wanted to make a profit using someone else's strength without paying for it. Now that the laws say you cannot do that, so they decided to give a little wage that will not be said it is slavery, especially where it involves different races. Imagine where people have the same qualification doing the same job, but getting different rates.

Although the first Christianity came to North Africa in the 1st century AD, this was introduced by Mark the Evangelist in 60 AD, IN Alexandria on the Egyptian coast BY Mark who came from Jerusalem, from North Africa the gospel spread to other parts of Africa such as Ethiopia. During the reign of Constantine Christianity was recognised as official language. So North Africa was one of the communities who were the first in the world to receive Christianity.

However, the culture of Africa is varied and manifold consisting of a mixture of cultures with various tribes that each have their own unique characteristic from the continent of Africa. It is a product of diverse populations that inhabit the continent of Africa and the African diaspora. African traditions are expressed through music, dance and sculpture, this is deeply ingrained in to the whole African culture. The African continent is bounded between the Mediterranean

Sea, the Red Sea, the Indian Ocean and the Atlantic Ocean. Africa has over 54 different unique countries with over 3000 diverse tribes. Kenya offers the best of Africa on show, from the best wild life in its National Parks, to the beautiful Diani Beach, Kenya offers the best of everything. Places with spectacular views, pristine beaches and amazing cultural mix and delicious cuisine. African Culture rich and diverse culture across the vast continent – the Victoria Falls Guide. In the African culture the "self" is not separate from the world, it is united and intermingled with the natural and social environment. There is a relationship between one's community and the surroundings that an individual becomes one of the groups, whose decision and action affects the entire group [.

Some of the things that are in the African cultures are making the Europeans doubt the sincerity of their Christianity, which makes it appear to be moving in two different ways.

19

Religion as Justification

The emergency of colonies in the Americas and the need to find labourers was the time that the Europeans turn their attention to Africa where they would get slaves as free labour the process of having free labour made them to have wealth without any loss, maximising their profits.

By just looking at it, it can be seen how it flourished, because by getting free labour they could have to make good profits, that is why the Trans-Atlantic Slave Trade grew. The three main reasons that grew the demand for African Slaves were; cultural, demographic, and economic foundations of the Atlantic Slave Trade. Africans would sell each other as punishment for a crime, as payment for a family debt, the most common was that, if there was war and the other nation is defeated, they could be sold as slaves, so as the trade flourished people were kidnapping each other and selling them, Christopher Columbus likely transported the first slaves in the 1490s on his expedition to the Island of Hispaniola, now Haiti and the Dominican Republic. Most of the African slaves were used for heavy labour. Sometimes the European people are so addicted in accumulating wealth to the extent *that* they do not even care what it means to your health as long as it enriches them. That is why there was this selling of people across the Atlantic buying people from Africa, shipping them across the Atlantic to go and make them work in plantations in America. These people became very rich because they had free labour. Now the whole thing is happening, but in a hidden way, they are justifying themselves that the labourers are being paid, but it is not proportional, the labour that was put in there, the profits, and the wedges paid, the slavery is now hidden.

Modern Day Slavery

There is still modern-day slavery in so many different forms risking human rights across the supply chain. This is disregarding all the antislavery laws that are in place. This is taking place as human trafficking, the use of violence, coercion to transport, recruit or harbour people in order to transport for purposes such as forced prostitution, labour criminality and forced marriages and or organ mutilation. There are an estimate twenty one million to forty five million people trapped in this or in some form of slavery such as today, they have found a very tactful way of enslaving people, in some cases, just pretending to be paying yet when compared to the profits made, today there is a modern day slavery which means, although slave trade was abolished, it is now being practised in a tactful and hidden way. People are made to work for a very small amount of money, regardless of the huge profit made by the organisation. It is a well-known fact that some people are living below the poverty line. though as slaves. Modern day slavery is forced marriage forced labour where victims are made to work through violence and intimidation. Some examples of modern-day slavery are:

- sex trafficking
- child sex trafficking, child sexual exploitation; forced marriage domestic servitude including cleaning and forced labour, physical sexual and emotional abuse.

- forced labour: Forced labour is the most common element of modern slavery. the most extreme form of people exploitation. It is mostly associated with forced labour slavery with physical violence, infect the ways people are forced to work are more (insidious) one of the scariest and most difficult to change (ingrained) in some cultures. Slavery is when someone owns you like a piece of property (servitude) subjected to someone more powerful is similar to slavery. You might live on the person's premises work for them and be unable to leave, but they do not own you. Forced labour mean you are forced to do work that you are not agreed to under the threat of punishment.
- Bonded labour or debt bondage: Debt bondage exists when labourers (sometimes with their families) are forced to work for an employer in order to pay off their own debts or those they have inherited. The victims of debt bondage, if they try to leave, are usually caught and returned by force.

Morden day governments should not allow domestic servitude because people are treated inhumanly, yet all human life should be treated the same.

Every child who is still under the age of 18 are classed as children, therefore by law they should be under the guardian of someone over 18, if they are made to work, it is called forced child labour.

- unlawful recruitment and use of child soldiers.
- people little to secure their compliance.

Modern day slavery takes a whole range of types of exploitation, some of these happen together, the phone number of modern-day slaveries is 08000121700 and the web site is: Modern day slavery destroys lives, damages communities and has strong links with organised crimes, Victims are always deceived or coerced into abusive situations that they feel they are unable to leave. It is a hidden crime; it is a complex and multifaceted problem which requires us to work together to fight the problem. In every situation, no matter how bad it would be there is always some good that can be found in all those bad things such as in slave trade. Slave trade was benefitting them in that they were getting cheap labour or free labour. There were some who were fighting to get it abolished, but then, a revolution cannot take place in a day. In 1863, January 1, this is the time when Lincoln was president of America, the first slaves were set free with some resistance from the hard-hearted ones, because they knew that their way of getting free labour was being closed, and no more getting rich through using some one's blood and thinking that it was a God given opportunity. Abolitionists were working day and night to have it abolished. It was even argued that the favourable trade winds from Africa *to* the Americas were evidence of this (providential) protective care of God's design. When people want some changes to happen, they are no longer revolting as they used to be, but now people have decided to talk and get things changed in a peaceful way. But doing it this way, sometimes takes longer to get a change. Revolution does not take place in a day. Christianity played a vital role in the abolishing of slave trade after a long time of debate. There were a lot of beatings, cruelty and mistreatment of slaves by slave masters. When slave trade was at its peak, when slave owners were making maximum profits, there were some who sympathised with these slaves that they were fighting for it to be abolished. Slavery was carried out mostly during the period of 1680-1780. There are some who sympathised with slaves, and did not take that lightly. Now that they fought for the abolishing of slavery, people have decided to go underground. People are made to work harder for a very small wage/ salary regardless of how much profit that organisation is making, very unproportioned disregarding how much production they have brought into the organisation. People fought hard to liberate people from slavery. Christians are still urged that the battle is not yet over there are so many slaves now under the slavery of Satan. There are so many people still suffering today through the fault, not of their own. Enslaving of the people is now hidden. Christians are sitting and watching and doing nothing about it. We are grateful for the abolition of slave trade in 1823. It appears no one is looking into it anymore since people are now made to work modern slavery, which is a hidden way to make people think that there is no more slavery. People are made to work for so little that they cannot make a living, yet the companies concerned may be boasting of having so many million pounds profit every year. Do they ever take into consideration that these people were also created in the image of God, and that they also deserve a decent living standard?

One of the worst things slavery could do was that if the slave master was attracted to a slave woman, he could do what he wanted with the woman regardless of what the slave husband would feel or say. We still have the same situation today of people who happen to be managers or directors of organisations who, if they are attracted by some ladies in the company, they take them to be their wives regardless of the fact that they are married, just because they happen to work for their families, and that those managers are in a position of power, hence they abuse that position. With the fact that they hold that position women are unable to say no to them so they take advantage, oh! God help us, we are far from you.

British slave trade officially ended in 1807, making the buying and selling of slave's illegal; however, slavery itself had not ended. It was not until 1 August 1834 that slavery ended in the British Caribbean following legislation passed the previous year. Some slave owners were not happy, because, before they had free labour, maximising their profits on someone's blood.

However, (Genesis 9:24-27) (NIV), this verse has been wrongly used to support racial prejudice and slavery. Noah's curse was not directed towards any particular race but to the Canaanite nation- a nation God knew would become wicked. The curse was fulfilled when the Israelites entered the promised land, they drove the Canaanites out, "see the book of Joshua". (NIV) (Genesis 21:9-10) (NIV) (Exodus 20:10, 17) (NIV) This teaches us that if someone appears to be blessed more than you, do not hate that person because God knows everyone of us, He knows the day He will bless you, or He knows what blessings He will give you which are different which are different from those you may be emulating because God gives us different gifts, just praise Him and give all the glory to Him when you see that He has blessed others, yours is coming. Sometimes we miss out on God's gift because when he is preparing it for us, we run into conclusion and take out what has not been prepared for us. Elsewhere in this book it says Jesus' dos not like to see anyone oppressed, so where is the justification of saying God condones slavery, (Luke 4:18) Jesus' mission on earth was for the poor and the oppressed so if you are enslaving or oppressing other people, you are doing things against the will of God, sometimes, we must ask Him to reveal these things to us so that we do not do things that offend Him, (NIV). Sometimes when we want to justify our misdeeds, we refer to the scripture, because with scripture anyone can bring their interpretation even though there is no divine revelation in it. How do the two things Mary that He condone slavery and at the same time He does want see any one oppressed, this has to be looked into deeply how we can come up to be able to speak with one voice on this matter? (Exodus 22:21-24) The Lord was teaching His people to be perfect telling them that whatever bad thing they do to other people, they may suffer the same fate. He reminded them that, they should not enslave other people they should know that they were once slaves in a foreign land sometime. What people do not realise is that what happened to other people would happen to them as well. For example, those who are widows did not want their husbands to die, if they would mistreat the widows and the orphans, then the Lord would do the same to them and their wives would be widows as well and their children orphans as well. The Lord's eye is watching the widows and the orphans His ear is listening to their cry. So, please do not arouse the anger of the Lord, because when He reacts it will be a disaster on you. God is teaching on how we should treat others for we may be treated with the same treatment, that we use to treat others. some clergy tried to push the idea that it was possible to be a good slave master and Christian at the same time, and pointed to St. Paul's Epistles which called for slaves to obey their masters, *and St.* Peter's letter, although they claimed that these slaves were being brought to America to be made to receive Christianity, no missionary work was carried out amongst them to prove the point that they were brought there for that purpose. This shows that the argument was just a cover of whatever deeds they were carrying out, so that excuse does not carry weight at all. (1 Peter 2:18-25) (NIV) The writer was clear and straightforward in this epistle, he was telling us to emulate Jesus who was accused of faults not His own, but He never fought back. He said slaves you did not choose to be slaves, but be happy that you are following Christ's footsteps. There is nowhere he said masters be cruel to your slaves. He is saying, you should not give them an excuse, you must be found to be as clean as your Saviour. The goal is to win every soul to Christ we should win those cruel masters to Christ. Jesus died for all our sins, let us receive that and be saved, Jesus paid for it all.

There was a division among Christians, some saying it was Biblical for Christians to be slave owners while some were saying it was evil. This shows clearly the contrast that is there between the earthly kingdom and the heavenly kingdom. Christians are expected to value human life and always remember that man was created in the image of God. What a contrast, Jesus came for the oppressed, (Luke 4:18) (NIV) unfortunately with us, instead of standing for the oppressed, it us who are the oppressors, are we near Jesus? If we are, we must explain which way we are like Jesus, if not it is time, we revisit ourselves. This must not be an outward display, but just a heartfelt kind of feeling.

On the other hand, we are only learning of the Americans

enslaving the African people and being cruel to them, where did that spirit of selling your brother come from. Were these people selling their biological brothers, or for fathers would you be selling your biological sons, we hear the story of the abolishing of slave trade coming from one side of the Atlantic, had not been for the abolishing from that side, does it mean that the African population could still be selling slaves to this date? What surprises is that to this date is that, people are drowning in seas crossing in small boats risking their lives running away from their fellow African rule, comparing between the two evils. It appears, the African rulers have paid no attention to it, have not bothered to look into the matter to find out why this is so happening and try to find the root cause and try to put it right and eradicate the root cause. But this is going on and on unchecked and there is no sign of any solution in sight, when is the wind of change going to blow so we can see so many lives being saved? This should bring us a realisation and start to think about how do we value human life.

The Bible Was Used to Justify Slavery

Although there are some people who fought for the freedom of slaves, there are some who died in slavery and never saw that freedom, the Lord knows what to do with their souls. There were some preachers like Rev. Jaymes Robert Moony who would preach pointing to the grave yard, knowing that there were some who never saw the freedom. Being touched in spirit when preaching, sometimes he pictures the graveyard- that is where his congregation was born. It was called Georgia cemetery, this name, he has been told, for in this place the enslaved were stolen from before being sent to work the fields at Huntsville, Ala. The graveyard was where they buried their loved ones. It was there they could gather in private. It was there where they could worship a God who offered not only salvation, but the thing they sought most- the promise of freedom. That graveyard and those who founded what is now St. Bartley Primitive Baptist Church in 1820, was looking closely and being sympathetic to the young minister who then was leading the gathering of Christians. It is not lost on him that the gospel he preaches, the gospel so many African Americans embrace to sustain them through the horrors of beatings, and rapes, separation and lynching, separate and unequal, is the same gospel used to enslave them.

That is the history of the black church.

20

The Inconsistency
of Human Nature

Humans are known by being inconsistency, sometimes when they find that hard times are with them, they do not want to own up and say sorry, they want to pretend that they are always right, hence they are inconsistency in their promises, they retreat and not stand on their promise or their word. A human being is inconsistent in nature you might put your really love and trust in a human being, but still their behaviour might change. The inability to think for one's self weak reasoning and not knowing exactly what the creator wants, yet we should rely on the creator to know exactly what we should do sometimes we have to rethink of the right thing. Human nature itself has got some second thought here and there, the human brain fluctuates and is prone to changing things sometimes our brains are divided between two ideas. Inconsistent behaviour is behaviour that is unpredictable irregular or illogical to the situation. Human nature is normally selfish always wanting to satisfy your own needs first, by being selfish you are not behaving normally. A human being has, mental physical, and spiritual characteristics that will make us uniquely well. The inconsistence of human nature is that you cannot rely on human nature, because the trust you might put on them is not how they may behave, to your dismay. Human nature is full of pride and prejudice, and with the fact that a human being is living in a corrupt world, may be prone to corruption. You may put all your trust in them, but they may change suddenly and take the unexpected mood, and you are left in the cold. A human has got a behaviour that is always unpredictable. A human is always inconsistent because of the neurocomputation due to variability in the neural computation variability.

Human Nature is Full of Pride

When God gives us gifts, we tend to be proud of them thinking that it was something of our own making. We have to bear in mind and know that God gave us those gifts in order for His work to be accomplished. Human nature has got inbuilt pride by evolution because it served an important function for our foraging ancestors. We evolve to feel pride because of it serves an important social function. Pride is often considered a negative force in human existence – the opposite of humility and a source of human friction, when we get praises, we tend to get carried away and start putting the glory on ourselves instead of giving the glory to the creator of human beings. The characteristics of human nature are that it can be influenced by society to which it subscribes. Sometimes we forget that it may be a blessing to have an achievement then we may start boasting about it, yet if it is like that you have to be grateful about it. Do not be too proud of an achievement because sometimes pride goes before a fall. We know we work in order to have possessions, but sometimes they will make us to be proud, which we must try to guard against. Some achievements may lead to a sense of being superior to everyone, thus leading to pride, this can be avoided if we know that it is only luck, you are not better than everyone. Always try to use the word pride in a good sense, in order to avoid misusing it. Most of the time it is used in a negative way as one that has an unduly high opinion of one's self. Try always to be on the positive side of pride, since it has positive and negative depending on how you are using it. Do not chose the down side of pride but the upper side, although it forces us to take the down side.

Slavery in Africa

History of Slavery in Africa

The selling of slaves was widespread in Africa in the ancient world, was what was called the trans-Sahara trade connecting with the Indian Ocean slave trade in the early 16th century. If you owed someone and you are unable to repay it that person would sell you as a slave. If wars were fought and you are conquered, you were bound to be sold, so that is how slave trade was flourishing in Africa. Slavery in North Africa was dating back as far as ancient Egypt. The new kingdom 1558-1080 BC brought in slaves as prisoners of war, these were bought in large numbers. They were used as domestic workers and in the most difficult labour mostly supervised labour. This flourished mostly in the Nile Region.

Whenever someone owed someone some money and being unable to pay it back, that debtor could be sold as a slave, or when a tribe fought with another tribe and was conquered, they could be sold as slaves, or prostitution or criminals all these were the factors that led to slave trade. The trans-Atlantic Slave trade was started by the Portuguese who went to buy people from West Africa and sold them as slaves to America. This is where slavery has been blackened because these Portuguese either they bought these or kidnap them. This is where the root of sin is because this is done against their wish of the people, anything done against the wishes of anybody is a great sin. Because these people were sold to America to work in the sugar plantations, tobacco fields, mining, timber, coffee, and coco plantations, so they were used as tools, so the owners could make big profits because they were using free labour. That is the reason why slavery is still practised today, in a hidden way because people want to make profit on others, it is because they tasted getting labour freely. They are now very tactful not to be detected. They used to kidnap people and selling them as slaves or taking them back to Europe as slaves. In 1619. A Portuguese slave ship, called Sao Joao Bautista went across the Atlantic Ocean half full with its cargo was mostly human cargo; captured Africans from Angola in South Western Africa.

The Trans-Atlantic slave trade of global slave trade transported between 10 to 12 million enslaved Africans across the Atlantic Ocean to the Americas from the 16th to the 19th century.

Slave trade was abolished in the United States of America from January 1 1808. However, some slaving continued on an illegal basis for the next fifty years. Slave trade took about 400 years.

Course of evince do not in a day but it takes some time, on January 1 in 1863 president Lincoln formerly issued the emancipation Proclamation, calling on the Union Army to liberate all enslaved people in states still in rebellion as some states and some individuals were trying to resist that law. This threatened to split the unity that was there within the states, but as time went, everyone complied and the states kept their unity. There were as many as three million slaves who were freed that time. The abolition of slave trade was enacted in 1808 but the resistance went on until 1863.

The Act prohibiting the importation of slaves, the 1808 Act imposed heavy penalties on international traders, but did not end slavery itself, nor the domestic sale of slaves. Who was the last slave? Sylvester Magee, claimed May 29 1841 -October 15, 1971, was believed to be the last living American slave. He received much publicity and was accepted for treatment by the Mississippi Veterans Hospital as a veteran of the American Civil War.

Slavery in the United States ended in 1865, but in West Africa it was not legally ended until 1875, and then it stretched unofficially until almost World War 1.

Britain was the most dominant between 1640 and 1807, when

the British slave trade was abolished. It is estimated that Britain transported 3.1 million Africans (of whom 2.7 million arrived) to the British colonies in the Caribbean North and South America and to other countries.

A bill passed by congress on January 31 in 1865, and ratified on December 6 in 1865, the 13th amendment abolished slavery in the United States of America.

Modern Slavery

Modern slavery is a multibillion-dollar industry with just the forced labour aspect generating US$150 billion each year. The global slave index 2018 estimates that, roughly 40.3 million individuals are currently caught in modern slavery, with 71% of those being female, and 1 in 4 being children.

Armed conflicts, state sponsored, forced labour, and forced marriages were the main causes behind the estimated 9.2 million Africans who live in servitude without the choice to do so, according to Global Slave Index of 2018.

So, the slave trade that flourished in America had some factors and some roots of it, it did not just happen.

It appears most of the slaves came from Africa during that time. It also appears during the modern-day Africa is still lagging behind in its development why? This has to be looked into and to start doing something to correct the imbalance. The majority of the enslaved people in the new world came from West Central Africa before 1519, all Africans carried into the Atlantic disembarked at Old World ports, mainly Europe and the offshore Atlantic Islands.

As of 2018, the countries with most slaves were: India (8 million), China (3.86 million), Pakistan (3.19 million), North Korea 2.64 million), Democratic Republic of the Congo (1 million), Nigeria 1.9 million), Indonesia (1.22 million, Russia (794 000) and the Philippines 784 000).

Transatlantic Slave Trade

There are two factors that cause slavery, and those who are practising it take advantage of the primitivity of the people and that some people are cruel at heart This trade proved to be big business those days because of the primitivity of the people that time or the cruelty of some people, who if there was no law, they could still be doing it to this date disregarding the fact that humans were created in the image of God. The Transatlantic Slave Trade not only distorted Africa's economic development, but it also distorted views of the history and importance of African continent itself. It is only in the last fifty years that it has been possible to redress this distortion to begin to re-establish Africa's rightful place in world history.

Abolition

Christian Abolitionists

During the time of slavery, it was well established in the minds of those who practised slavery that it was the backbone of the economy, that is, they could maximise their profit because labour was free. This has gone into the DNA of those who were doing it, such that it is encoded in such a way that when the laws were passed to abolish it, the law was on paper only not in their DNA. Now it is seen being practised in a way that it is never noticed, as it appears, it might go on for some time until when the divine powers intervene. Christians must not get tired for this is what Jesus commissioned them when He said, therefore go and make disciples, Jesus knew that there would be such a thing as this we are facing today. The reason why Christianity wanted to see all slaves freed is that slavery is dehumanising slaves were treated like they were not human beings, all their dignity was taken away from them. Because of the resistance from those who were proslavery is the reason it took a long time to abolish. The resistance persists to this present day, when some proslavery are doing it under cover, appearing like they love those they are enslaving. Those who are doing it today are mixing Christianity and technology, wanting everyone to believe that they are being love when in actual case they are being enslaved. To show that slavery is cruel, some slaves tried to escape, but if they were unluck and they got caught, the punishment was death, because they wanted to make that as an example so that no other slave would ever think of escaping as well. Most of the slaves knew that the churches taught that God wants them to be free, so most of the slaves joined Christianity because of wanting freedom from slavery. Sometimes people tend to have their thinking determined by the environment that even Christians that time did not have a deep conviction that a slave had a human soul as well and that human soul in the master, the soul in the slave is the same as the soul in the master. So, those slaves who had joined Christianity although they were still enslaved, their hopes were kept alive by Christianity, this evil that was practised persist in the peoples' minds to this day because racism is still showing its ugly face. Those elements who have slavery mind in them want Christianity to die first then they will enslave people without anyone voicing. Everyone these days were basing their expectations by equating the hidden slavery that is there today to the story of the Exodus in the Old Testament where God through Moses delivered the children of Israel from Egypt. The prayer is, the power is yours Lord if you did it before to the Hebrew children, you can still do it again.

To make sure that they do not revolt, they could not go anywhere without the owner's permission, because where ever they would be going the owner would first make sure there was at least one white person to see and know what they were doing, they were not allowed to carry any firearms in case they would revolt against the white masters, they were not to be taught to read or write, knowing that knowledge is power, because if they know they would one day ask for their freedom. This shows that even though they were trying to base their argument on the Bible they knew that what they were doing was against the will of God. What these people who love to make other people slaves is that they do not know that they are slaves of Satan being given evil thoughts by the devil you are a slave. Jesus came to liberate us from those thoughts but we are refusing, enslaving ourselves. Before the coming of Christianity Muslim and Judaism, people were worshiping many gods. Churches should not rest for there is still a lot to do to ensure that this hidden slavery is eradicated and we all become the children of God. The family of slaves were not the same, sometimes the father could be owned by one owner and the wife and children could be owned by the other owner or if they were lucky, father, mother and the children could be owned by one owner, so the family of slaves was stable. While some clergymen were using Christian scriptures to justify their sins on slavery, they found themselves doing the wrong thing but want the Bible to support their sin, which the Bible cannot do, it will keep on being the Bible as it was before and will still be. True Christians were interpreting the Bible as it should be and kept on doing the right thing of scouring the Bible to end slavery and they should not rest because slavery is continuing under cover. Although evangelicals tend to receive most of the credit for this, the origin of Christian abolitionism can be traced to the late 17th and the religious society of Friends or Quakers.

Inconsistences

It would be wrong to suggest that there were Christian saints and sinners in regards to slavery. It can be argued that both characteristics coexisted within denominations and individuals alike, demonstrating the way of thinking peculiar to an individual (idiosyncrasies) and inconsistence of all human beings.

This was also the situation with other denominations. The Church of England being the established church, had links to slavery through the united society for the propagation of the gospel missionary organisations, which had plantations in Barbados, while the Bishop of Exeter was a personal slave owner. Moreover, Anglicans involved in slavery often poured in their ill-gotten gain into church coffers. And in cities such as Bristol, the church bells pealed when Wilberforce's Anti-Slave Trade Bills were defeated in parliament.

However not all Anglicans were complicated. Beilby Porteous the bishop of London was an evangelical abolitionist whose sermons regularly railed against slavery. Similarly, the Clapham sect, a group of Anglicans based around Clapham, South London carried out sterling work to end slave trade.

Comment

According to the foregoing story, it appears there is not yet that brotherly love coming from the bottom of our hearts which compels us that we are children of the same God. Jesus' blood that was spilt at Calvary was to save everyone gentile or Jew, slave or master. Paul was given an assignment for the gentiles which he did and brought the gentiles to the fold. Although the slave trade was ended, it is like ending the slave trade is one thing, and practicing slavery is another. Slavery is still being practiced in our hearts; Paul did not condone slavery. During the time of Jesus, slavery was being practiced, Jesus left slavery being practiced, but we are taking this as an excuse. At the conversion of Paul, Jesus said Paul is my vessel, which means he was being prepared to go and dismantle slavery, so there is no excuse on our part, of basing our argument on what Jesus did. (Ephesians 2:14-18) (NIV) Jesus was crucified in order to break the barriers that divided us into Romans, Gentiles, or Jews so that we become one, there is a need for us to become one in Christ. The Jews regarded themselves as the chosen people, but disregarded the gentiles as the chosen people. So, anything that was done by the gentile could not carry any weight according to the Jews. Yet according to the task that was given to Paul, there is no poor or rich, no slave or master, all are the children of one Father. The author is pleading with the reader to say let us unite in Christ and become brothers and sisters in Christ, but we cannot do that without the aid of the Holy Spirit who must guide us all our lives, there is that mentality of enslaving other people in our hearts. That must be washed from our hearts if we are to become true Christians, who realise that we are the temples of the Lord, this means that the Lord must be able to dwell in us, so that whatever we do will be guided by the Holy Spirit.

Slave owners did something that was not expected of Christians. To be called Christians is to be said you are following the footsteps of Christ, and emulating what Christ came to set as an example. If Christ set an example for us, why are we taking our own ways? Without hiding behind whether other races were cursed: or whether you found the slave trade going on, what is your own conviction, when you are enslaving your father's son or daughter. It is said we should worship God in truth and in spirit, how do you feel yourself to be profiting on someone's blood. Without anyone reminding you, you can clearly see the contrast that is there between the earthly kingdom and the heavenly kingdom. The heavenly beings treat each other as equals, because of their environment, the heavenly kingdom is not corrupted as the earthly kingdom.

21

The Story of Philemon

Taking Philemon's case, Paul could not be said to be condoning slavery because he showed that in Christ we are equals. Because he asked Philemon to treat Onesimus according to Christianity and not according to the law of slavery. The law of slavery then said the punishment for a runaway slave when caught was death. Paul asked Philemon to take Onesimus back, but as a brother this time. Here Paul dismantled slavery in a Christian way. This answers the question why Jesus left slavery in existence. Sometimes we fail to grasp that the Lord plans well ahead of time, who are we to interfere with His plans.

(1Peter 2:18-25) This scripture has been used by those Christians who want to justify their misdeeds, this scripture is misquoted by those who would like to be slave owners. Yet the scripture did not justify them at all, the scripture was saying if you have been made a slave against your will, follow Christ's example when He obeyed His tormentors yet He would have called ten thousand angels to set Him free. This does not say in any way those who were persecuting Christ were right, but that Christ submitted Himself, the scripture was saying, slaves, submit yourselves, not that slavery was good for you, but that do not judge them, but leave it to the Lord, who knows, you might win them to the Lord one day. The scripture made it clear, in fear of the Lord, it is saying, be good all your life no matter who you are dealing with even to those who think bad of you think good of them that is what it means to be a Christian. Whatever suffering you are going through, know that the Lord also suffered for you, there is a vast difference between someone who is mistreated because they are wrong and someone who is mistreated because they have not done anything wrong. Some masters are harsh, some are gentle, but we are required to respond in the same way to both the masters, this is for our good not for their good, Christians be good in all walks of life. This scripture is teaching everyone to be human, it is not saying that people should enslave other people and treat them inhumanly. This scripture is meant for everyone not slaves only, not master only, but taking that everyone is a follower of Christ who gave us an example of how life should be lived on earth.

The Lord is never pushed to act in a rush, but does His work according to his plan. That is the reason why Jesus was in disagreements with the Pharisees who wanted Him to do things their own way. Jesus said I do things according to my Father who sent me. Look, Jesus came at a time when Israel was under the bondage of the Roman Empire, but after the resurrection, when He said He was going back, they even asked Him if He was leaving them under the York of the Romans. The same question was coming from those who were enslaved, especially those enslaved by fellow Christians, how would they feel? Do you know that Christ left that task to you and me? No stone should be left on top of the other. Paul did his part in dismantling slavery. Although Paul did not say any words that said slavery should be abolished, but the way he acted was saying that slavery was a sin which should not be entertained especially by Christians. The heavenly kingdom will not be established on earth, remember, a building will not be built if there are some stumps in the ground in which that building is going to be established, those stumps must be uprooted first. If they are not uprooted, when they start decaying, the building will collapse, or if they start having shoots the building will have cracks. For the kingdom to be established on earth let us be prepared to take each other as brothers in Christ. Those personal obstructions must be removed first, let us know that some of the things we are doing are making us to be far from the heavenly kingdom, collectively or individually. We always pry, your kingdom come, your will be done on earth as it is in heaven. It is time to examine ourselves, individually or collectively. Do we really deserve the heavenly kingdom to come? Let us ask to be transformed so as for us to deserve that kingdom to come. Christ did His part by going to the cross and His resurrection was His way of dismantling the things that made us to be far from Him, now it is left for you and me to do our part. (Ephesians 2:14-18) There were some barriers to the heavenly kingdom which were dismantled by those saints who came before us. Now this is left for you and me, but it appears we have gone some steps backwards instead of moving some steps forward. Christ is still with us in those trying times he will never leave us alone. (Colossians 3:11). The scriptures say clearly here that Philemon owned Onesimus yet no one should own a person, but God owns us all, and let us all be brothers in Christ. Here Onesimus was supposed to die because he had committed two crimes, to run away and to steal, by the law of slavery he was worth for death, yet Paul said to Philemon, take him back as a brother this time. For us to be followers of Christ we must take this story seriously for it means something in our Christian life. There are so many barriers in our life that are separating us from getting closer to Christ, there are so many barriers in life that are separating us from getting closer to Christ, we pray, God help us to break those barriers in order for us to see you Lord.

22

Bible of Oppression and Liberation

The Africans who were brought to America from 1619 onward carried with them diverse religious traditions. What does it mean to say that the Africans who were brought to America during or from 1619 onwards, carried with them diverse religious traditions? This means that there are significant differences in religious beliefs and practice. About 20 t0 30 percent were Muslim, Pierce said some had learned of Christianity before coming to America. But many practised African spiritual traditions. Earlier on, many slave holders were not concerned with the spiritual wellbeing of Africans. But few had qualms about using Christianity to justify slavery. They were not concerned with spiritual well-being of the Africans. They used Christianity to justify slavery, even some Biblical scholars could just follow what was happening without seeking any guidance from the Lord. We must always seek guidance other than walking unguided. They could interpret the Bible the way that would justify their deeds, but not the reality. The reality is that, the Lord treats every human being as equals: no stone on top of the other. There were some preachers who would have a smoke screen pretending to encourage slave owners to allow their slaves to attend services, yet those services were attended separately, making slaves to sit in the back of the church. Shamelessly, quoting Ephesians 6:5 out of context because it did not say anything to justify their deeds. If someone pleads with you to do your work faithfully, it is for the Lord not to please a human being. Whatever we are doing in life is for the Lord and not for anybody at all.

Some theologians said it was providence that had brought Africans to America as slaves, since their enslavement would allow them to encounter Christian and thus their eternal souls would be saved, said Mark Noll, a Historian of American Christianity.

Some preachers encouraged some slave owners to allow their slaves to attend worship services-though only in separate gatherings led by white proslavery preachers. They had to be seated in the back or balcony of segregated church. These men of God argued that the sermon on the injunction in Ephesians and Colossians "Slaves obey your earthly Masters" would promote (docility) submissiveness among enslaved.

Washington's Museum of the Bible displays "A Slave Bible" Published in 1807 which removed portions of scripture including the exodus story that could inspire rebellious thinking.

Sessions cites Bible passage used to defend slavery in defence of separating immigrant families:

Some ministers promoted the idea that Africans were the descendants of Ham, cursed in the book of Genesis and thus their enslavement was fitting.

That Biblical interpretation is made up of whole cloth in the 15th century" Noll said. There is just no historical record of any seriousness to back it up. It is made up, at a time when Europeans are beginning to colonise Africa. Slaveholders frequently noted that the Israelites of the Old Testament owned slaves. They refer to the Israelites of Old Testament, saying that they owned slaves, but He is the same God who said, "I have heard the crying of my children because they are in slavery in Egypt and I have come down myself to rescue them". Do they want Him to come down to them as well? The Lord expects everyone to learn a lesson when He sets up an example. At creation He did the real creation, but He does not keep on doing the same, but mankind is multiplying. Do they want the Lord to keep on coming down? He expects us to have taken a lesson here. In the present day, how is the relationship between slave and master, or manager and employee? The slave master could just take a woman he wanted without taking into consideration that the woman was married to a slave, just because the husband had no power. Managers today are taking women at will regardless of their marriage just because those women are looking for favours, shame to society, "Lord help us".

Abolitionists tried to make arguments against using the Bible to justify slavery, but they were in the minority. God works in mysterious ways, because, although they were in the minority, they were successful in their efforts to do what is good, so they were heard and slavery was abolished. Today we expect the Lord to do His will and things might change. They were considered to be "radical", it was said. And often they were considered to be the unbelieving (infidels,) because how could they say God was opposed to slavery if it was so obvious in the Bible that He was not". The foremost objectors, of course, were African Americans themselves. Large numbers adopted the faith, and they quickly began remaking it into their own. The African showed that if there was someone to help you, be strong and be of good courage. When there were some white abolitionists, they were encouraged to know that they were helping people who deserved to be helped, because they were appearing that the help was good for them because they were also involved

Currently, slavery seems to have gone under cover, it is also required that there be a divine spirit that goes to uncover and let it be known that the evil that is found in slavery is still there. As soon as enslaved people learned to read English, they immediately began to read the Bible, and they immediately began to protest this idea of a biblical justification for slavery" Pierce said, "Literally as soon as black people took pen paper, we are arguing for our own liberation."

Abolition, Anti-Slavery movements, and the rise of sectional controversy. Black and white abolitionists in the first half of the 19th century waged a biracial assault against slavery. Their efforts heightened the rift that had existed. It proved to be very effective because both sides were in one accord.

It is interesting to note that there were people like William Wilberforce who really had a call and was bold enough to go to parliament with his calling. We know that we have a God of yesterday, today, and is a God of tomorrow, we ask Him to do it again, this time on the undercover slavery, because it appears now it requires divine intervention. It is interesting to note that there are so many Christians who now believe that there should not still be any slavery existing to this present day. But there is the inconsistence of human nature, who still believe that separation of the races who believe that when it is said a man was made in the image of God, it was meant for a certain race and there is a race that is excluded from that phrase. The way slaves were treated and the way they are treated takes away all human dignity. It is said, a man was created in the image of God, so the way they were treated does not portray the image of God. How natural is slavery a natural thing, when all the dignity that was put on man by God has been taken away. Are we dealing with two separate issues, the neutrality of slavery or the imagery of a man put in human by God? An argument that slaves are a low grade of people that they deserve to be treated that way. You will find that sometimes it may be crafted by man in such a way that these slaves will be deprived of that opportunity. In the end they are said they were naturally born like that when it was a deprivation that was cleverly imposed on them. The argument mentioned above is the one that is making it difficult for this modern-day slavery because some people will think that they are doing them a service when they are not. We have already mentioned that what appears to be voluntary slavery is not voluntary, but only that it was crafted in the first place.

We may try by all means to justify slavery by putting some covering, but as long as it is something "forced" then it becomes difficult to justify. When people have a free will to choose, that means they are able to take the best they can, other than things being imposed on them. Things that are done on free will tend to be done correctly, then those that you do unwillingly. What they choose to do from their free will, they tend to do it responsibly, and sometimes comes out to be the original.

From Noah's curse to slavery's rationale

Before the 17th century, people did not think of themselves as race. Sometimes one bad thing begats another, the slave trade began the race thing, I do not know what they wanted to make a difference by race if it was not there before the idea of race began to evolve in the late 17th century after the beginning of European exploration and colonisation, as a folk ideology about human differences associated with different populations, Europeans, Americans and Africans- brought together in the new world. Race was brought in as a categorising term referring to human beings. Was used in the English language in the late 16th century. Until the 18th century, it a generalised meaning similar to other classifying terms such as type sort or kind. A new survey found differences between black and white adults in their views on racial discrimination, barriers to African progress. The modern-day use of the term "race" is a human invention. The world got along without race for the over whelming majority of its history. The term "race" was used infrequently before the 1500s, was used to identify groups of people with a kinship or group connection. The modern-day use of the term "race" is a human invention. Now it is used to describe and categorise people into various social groups based on characteristics like skin colour and fascial features and genetic hereditary. Race is not a valid biological concept, is a real social construction that gives or denies benefits or gifts or privileges

As the stories go, this one has all the elements of good soap opera: nudity, sex and dysfunctional families.

For many scholars, though, the enigmatic tale in Genesis 9 describing how Noah cursed the descendants of his son Ham with servitude remains a way to explore the complex origins of the concept of race: how and why did people begin to see themselves as racially divided?

In the Biblical account, Noah and his family are not described in racial terms, but as the story echoed through the centuries, and around the world, variously interpreted by Islamic Christianity and Jewish scholars, Ham came to be widely portrayed as black: blackness, servitude and the idea of racial hierarchy became inextricably linked.

By the 19th century, many historians agree, the belief that African-Americans where descendants of Ham were a primary justification for slavery among Southern Christians.

If Ham the cursed son of Noah is the one who later became an African, was he originally the same colour as his brothers? If that was the case, then there must have been a time of transformation, from the colour of his brothers to the African colour.

We cannot just take the story and just present the conclusion without explaining. Since we are able to tell people that Ham is the cursed son of Noah, we must be able to tell that from the three biological brothers how he transformed into black, and how long was the transition. Where ever these brothers were that time, when he migrated from that place to settle in Africa since we have decided to give an account let us give a traceable account. We cannot give a history half way and leave the rest for people to be grappling their way

If many Africans are slaves let us just take it that way and not mixing with the curse of Ham, let us keep them separate issues. It is not disputed that Ham was cursed, let us be able to explain that he was cursed to what extent.

If we are taking this from the Bible, let us ask for a revelation, so that we give the correct interpretation, since scriptures were inspired by Him, He is able to give us a revelation.

23

Did God Allow Slavery?

aul was saying this when He was speaking spiritually, but otherwise people did not receive it spiritually. He was saying obey your earthly slave masters, for there to be no fighting on earth knowing that even those earthly masters have a master to be answerable to as well, the heavenly master. Every thinking Christian must think deeply and analyse. Proslavery Christians will always quote (Ephesians 6:5) where Paul says: "Slaves, obey your earthly masters with respect and fear, and with sincerity of heart, just as you would obey Christ. Obey them not to win their favour when their eye is on you, but as slaves of Christ, doing the will of God from your heart. Serve whole heartedly, as if you were serving the Lord, not people, because you know that the Lord will reward each one for whatever good, they do whether they are slave or free. I do not know where these slave owners got their justification from, Paul is saying, obey them not to win them for favours, but just as Christ obeyed His tormentors when He was being led to the cross. Slave masters were not spared by Paul because he also reminded them of the coming judgement, since they claimed to be Christians, he said to them, I plead with you, be warned before that day, so, they should know better of that coming day. The master in heaven will reward everyone according to their deeds. He told masters to treat their slaves with that day in mind, knowing that He cannot be bribed by any wealth, because everything on earth they claim to be theirs, are His, therefore, masters treat your slaves in the same way you would like your Father in heaven to treat you. Do not threaten them, since you know that he who is both their master and your self is in heaven, and there is no favouritism with Him."

According to the passage, Paul does not seem to condone or condemn slavery, but is saying as children of the same Father. If we are children of the same Father, can you make your father's son your slave? That is very impossible, on what grounds would you base such deeds? Paul tells masters and slaves to live in harmony as children of the same Father. In the church, everyone has freedom that they are denied by society. He says we have to be responsible in whatever we do, let Jesus be your supervisor at your place of work.

The reason why we need supervisors or masters is just because we are living in a corrupt world. In this corrupt world to be honest, you have to be forced to be honest. Yet in a divine world, everyone is their own supervisor or their own master.

When we say, your kingdom come: the Lord pauses the same question back to us and say: come from where, yet the kingdom is in your midst. Jesus said stay in Jerusalem, it is not only staying in Jerusalem for the sake of staying in Jerusalem, but stay in one accord in order to be able to receive the Holy Spirit.

It is up to us to choose whether we like to be forced to be honest or to be voluntarily honest so as to make our world good to live in.

Slave and Master

So, when Paul was saying, slaves obey your masters, he did not say owning a slave was permitted, but he said, every work we do here on earth is not for anyone but for Jesus. Do not claim to be masters here on earth for we all have one master who is in heaven.

Do not perform badly because you are an employee, that work is your work in Jesus' name. This brings us to the model prayer to which we say your kingdom come, yet Jesus says the kingdom is already among you, which means there is no point in keeping on asking, but to examine ourselves, and let us do the right thing.

Always do your work to the best you can, not because the master is not there, but Christ is there. No matter who you work for, or who works for you, always know that you are doing it to please your Father in heaven. We may be at different levels on earthly society, we are all equal in the eyes of God. Paul's letter to Philemon stresses the same point; Philemon the master and Onesimus the slave ended up being the same, because they were all brothers in Christ.

Where Paul says, "slaves obey your earthly masters" he is teaching people to be real Christians. He is saying, be like Christ who obeyed His tormentors as He was being led to the cross, it does not mean that His tormentors were right, yet Paul is saying follow His footsteps. Slave masters should not delude themselves and say that Paul has exonerated them, yet in that verse he is making them know that in the eyes of God they were the same as their slaves. Paul was quite clear here when he said, do not obey them in order to receive some favours from the earthly people who are also at the mercy of our Father in heaven. This obedience Paul speaks about is not to a human being but to our heavenly Father.

When he turned to the slave masters, he warned them not to take the place of God, but that they were at par with the slaves they thought they were their gods.

People have to be reminded that there is tomorrow coming when we will face judgement, being judged by the same God of all, who does not look at us as gentile, Jew, slave or master.

The reason why the author is concerned with Christians being slave masters, is the cruelty that was done to slaves by their handlers. That being done by those who claim to be Christians, leaves Christianity with a question mark. Jesus left to us pure Christianity; its purity was manifested at Pentecost. But this is now tainted by individuals

Christians' deeds which are contrary to pure Christianity. For this pure Christianity to be received requires us not to leave Jerusalem. When they did not leave Jerusalem, they were in one accord, which is very rare with today's Christianity.

Did so Many Christians Support Slavery?

Other than spending time on arguing what happened to Abraham or what happened to Noah, we have to take into account John 4:23-24 where it clearly states that God is Spirit those worship Him must worship Him in Spirit and in Truth. The same Jesus in Luke 4:18 says He came to set free those who are enslaved so when Jesus sets them free and you enslave them and you say it is biblical what Biblical without Jesus. Let us do our things in truth and in spirit. The reflection of the slave trade by the BBC gives us a review of the slave, it is a valuable opportunity to review the evils of Slave Trade. The Trans-Atlantic slave trade gives us time to assess its legacy. The Christian church was involved in slave trade, at many levels, in the first place, the church was the backbone of the slave trade, most of the slave traders and captains of slave ships were Christians. Sir John Hawkins was a Christian who brought slaves from Africa to America said his crew served God daily and loved one another, (in October 1562). These Christians taking slaves from Africa to America claim that they served God daily. These slaves they brought from Africa, were they coming on their own accord? If not, where is the justification of taking people against their will and you still say you are serving God.

The way we do Christianity has to be looked into, to see if we are really following the footsteps of Christ, or we are trying to make some amendments in Christianity to suit ourselves. Bear in mind that it was not all Christian who were doing that, there were some who played a vital role in its abolition. How can the church help itself and others on how to move forward? The Bible can always be used to support varying viewpoints, this is where we always ask to be given the divine revelation so we do not misinterpret and lead people astray. (Genesis 21:9-13) When Sarah saw that the son whom Hagar the Egyptian had borne to Abraham was mocking, her son Isaac, she said to Abraham, Sarah told Abraham to divorce the Egyptian slave woman, let her go with her son so that he does not take my son Isaac's inheritance. Then the matter distressed Abraham greatly because it concerned his son." But God said to him, "Do not be so distressed about the boy and your slave woman, listen to what Sarah tells you because it is through Isaac that your off springs will be reckoned. I will make the son of the slave into a nation also, because he is your offspring also."

So, the Christians who are proslavery are basing their arguments on the above happening, saying that God condoned slavery because Abraham had a slave. Even if they wanted to base their deeds on the scriptures, even without basing on the scripture, if they just look at it, how unjustly slaves were treated, would they say it was human according to them. Every human being has to be treated equally, the way you would like to be treated yourself. Let us not overlook the manner in which this family matter instructs us not to rest in outward privileges, or in our own doings. And let us seek the blessing of the new covenant by faith in its divine surety. Christian slave holders used the Bible to justify slavery. When asked, most would have defined themselves as Christians. They had two favourite texts: the Christian slave holders used to balance their religious beliefs with cruel facts of the peculiar institutions. Those who were proslavery wanted to strengthen their argument, wrote books to that effect, saying that enslaving people was biblical. These books use first-hand account to tell the story of slavery, for some of them, that rationalisation was right there in the Bible.

With the fact that the church supported the Trans-Atlantic Slave Trade, and also supporting the abolishing of Slave Trade, means that Christianity itself needs revisiting. That means in Christianity, we do not have Christians at heart but Christians at work. Christianity should be felt at heart not Christianity as an identity.

If some Christians were saying, being a slave master was Godly, and some Christians say it was not, that means they are not in one accord. If they are not in one accord, it means Christianity is still far from being spiritually filled. For the Holy Spirit to come down at Pentecost, they were in one accord. Christians, let us ask the Holy Spirit to dwell in us. Jesus said the comforter will be with you all your life to guide you and lead you into righteousness than to do it on your own. There is a vast difference between being spiritually filled and doing it in the flesh.

The title of this book is: "Contrast between the earthly kingdom and the heavenly kingdom" which means we are trying to see where these two differ, since we say "your kingdom come, and your will be done on earth as it is in heaven" this means we want life on earth to be as it is in heaven, so do we really mean that we want it to be like it is in heaven? It is for us to assess ourselves to see if what we are doing is like how it is done in heaven. Do we need anyone to tell us how far we are from heaven? The fact still remains that we want things to be like they are in heaven. It appears things are getting worse than they should be because everything appears to represent the earthly kingdom more than they should represent the heavenly kingdom.

Humans not to be Trusted

People cannot be trusted because they cannot stand on reality, when one changes their mind, it is like a house that is built on shaky ground which cannot hold any foundation. One who stands on the truth is relied upon, because that means they stand by their words, which is what everyone wants, the truth and nothing else. Untrustworthy damages relationships, you make promises and you break those promises, how will you be relied upon? There is deadline, but you miss the dead line, by doing so you cannot be relied upon.

What causes human beings not to be trusted, is that they do not keep their word, and that they do not want to take responsibility not able to die defending the truth they rather change statements, so how can they be trusted? It is human nature to have second thoughts that means that even if we agree on something you tend to have second thoughts and call them better ideas then you tend to have taken what has come as second thought disregarding the agreement you would have made with others, that is the reason why you cannot rely on human beings for they can be inconsistent. That is why it is said we should rely on the word from the Lord because He is consistent. Human beings are inconsistent when it comes to choosing simple things, that is why there was inconsistence during slave trade abolition, because others said it was biblical while others said it was not, yet those who were for the abolition were right because it is not godly to treat human beings cruelly as was done to slaves. That is the reason why during slavery Christians were taking different routes, because some had wrong interpretation, that is why we should ask for divine guidance because we cannot do it using blood and flesh.

(idiosyncrasies) meaning that people were created differently hence they behave differently. There could be some irrational choices from the same brain, otherwise showing that we are not spiritually filled to enable us to be consistent. Also, denominations may have different policies depending on who has the most influence when formulating the policies. That is why even to this day churches are still splitting because of the inconsistence of human beings; with that inconsistence they tend to have different choices hence taking the same thing differently it appears those splits in churches are still ongoing even for the foreseeable future.

The true interpretation of the Bible should be guided by the Holy Spirit, because originally it was inspired by the Holy Spirit, then, that should always lead to the correct interpretation of it. The Bible is always interpreted in such a way that it should support the idea of any one their ideas to be taken in order to suit their misdeeds. They could always quote from the Old Testament such as Exodus and Leviticus and say that they condoned slavery. When looking deeper and when analysing it will show that there was no such a thing. In the New Testament as well, they claimed that Paul condoned slavery because he said slaves obey your masters. If he had supported slavery, how then would he say treat slaves as brothers? It is because in Christianity we treat each other with brotherly love, not enslaving your brother and still claiming to be a Christian.

It is not yet known why slave trade flourished in in the African continent than in any other continents. If at all slave trade was not abolished and made illegal, could they still be selling slaves by now? What part did the African continent play in the abolishing of slave trade?

Slave trade had a devastating effect on the African Continent. Economic incentives for warlords and tribes to engage in slave trade promoted an atmosphere of lawlessness and violence. Depopulation and continuing fear of captivity made economic and agricultural development almost impossible throughout most of West African States.

They are practising slave trade in a hidden way today. People are drowning in seas these days trying to cross seas in small boats running away from African rule to seek voluntary slavery in overseas countries. When is this type of slave trade going to stop? It appears we have entered a certain revolution which needs rethinking. We cannot keep our old way of thinking when the times have turned a corner. The course of events is on another level, should we stay on the level we were before, food for thought.

Some chapters and verses in the Bible were always misquoted, it could be said that sometimes the forces of darkness may lead us to misquotation of the Bible. The devil will deal with your brain first and you are done. In order for the devil not to be detected, he will make you appear as if you were very intelligent. So, everything will be hidden behind intelligence. Some of the European countries are still entertaining the idea that Africans are slaves unto this day.

The truth about churches today is that they have not shifted much from their stance of slavery especially on different races, some churches today see no problem in owning slave to this date. Some Christian churches like the Quakers, the Presbyterians, the Methodists and the Baptists were against slavery but they were blamed by the Anglicans as non-conformists or dissenters because the churches were confused (bemuse) they disagreed with the beliefs and practices of the church of England. It appears we have not shifted a lot from that stance of those olden day churches. These churches were brave enough to keep on persisting until they had a victory. To those individuals who were proslavery, it appears they have not changed much because if you look at it, there is still a lot of proslavery in people's hearts Some individuals like Thomas Clackson worked hard for the abolition of slave trade and then it was legislated and it became law not to sell people as slaves.

During those days or even today people do not bother about asking for a revelation when reading the Bible, this means that we have to seek a clear revelation and to have a deep study of the Bible not to just take it at face value to be thoroughly analytic of it and get a true interpretation before misleading others into believing that this is what the Bible says when it is not what it is saying.

The Old Testament appears to Condone slavery sometimes, but a close look shows that God heard the cry of His sons and daughters in Egypt and came down to save them. Sometimes we tend to give the Lord a time frame of doing what we want, not knowing that He has got His own plans which are sometimes good for us in the long run. Let us remember that whatever happens, the Lord will always be on the throne. We may change our mind but the Lord endures for ever.

The church was involved in the Trans-Atlantic Slave Trade and the church was also involved in the abolition of slave trade. What is the legacy of such double standards and how is the church today going to help move forward? It may not be advisable to try to blame scriptures in such cases, they were inspired to stand for different purposes in our lives. But when interpreting them people tend to fit them where they cannot fit, while it is individuals who will try to make them suit their needs. In this case it is the interpretation of scriptures that is at play, and we have to be careful here not to lead others astray because of our misinterpretation.

When following closely the Trans-Atlantic slave trade, the Americans alone were not to blame. The African continent was also to blame because they were the ones who made these slaves to be readily available for sale. When uprooting a tree, we must start from the roots themselves, when we get rid of the roots it is to make sure that it will not sprout again, if we currently look at what is happening, people are preferring to go into voluntary slavery because they are sometimes finding life in Africa unbearable because of the type of rule that is coming out of Africa.

It is not a mistake to misinterpreted the Bible, but that we want it to suit our needs and our requirements. Where there are ten Individuals, we have ten different opinions, but that is not an excuse for miss-interpreting the Bible. All human beings are entitled to different opinions as long as those different opinions will make sense to what is on offer. Humans are inconsistent by design rocks mountains and the sun are consistent, infect so it may be pointed out that consistent things are dead, but God is consistent our God is alive. Inconsistence shows life in human beings, sometimes these different opinions will strive to change for the better. Some denominations during slave trade had different opinions, which means some were pro-slavery, where as some were abolitionists. This shows that it is peculiar to individuals as well as denominations.

The Church of England had links to slavery because it had plantations in Barbados. They used to bring in the ill-gotten money into the church, we may still have the same situation today, but that may now be done in a tactful way that some individuals may be bringing in their ill-gotten gains, but the church appears to accept. The church appears not yet spirit filled because it is bringing in a mixture of wealth and spirituality, since we are living in a corrupt world. To say we are living in a corrupt world should not be an excuse, in (Luke 4:18) (NIV) Jesus said He had come for the oppressed, and the church says it is following Jesus' so how can we oppress some in order to serve the oppressed, we must not make Christianity lose its saltness, it should remain the salt of the earth.

The city of Bristol had very strong link to slave trade, with such things having been done by the institutions that were expected to follow Christ's example, but were taking the opposite. Things happening that way, leaves a very unclean imprint that the church has a very big task, to try to make the image of the church a clean image to the people, it has to be known that the church today is there for the souls of those people, yet in cities such as Bristol, they celebrated and the church bell were ringing as a sign of happiness when Wilberforce's Anti-Slave Trade Bills were defeated in Parliament.

The reason why those who campaigned to abolish slavery won was because there were some people who never accepted what was being done by others to be cruel to human beings. They won because even in parliament although they are not all Christians there, there are some who are sympathetic at heart naturally, so those sided with the Christians, we still have such a situation today all the people cannot be hard hearted. The church has to see that there are some outside of the church who are better than those who go to church. The church has got to lead by example, not to be led by non-church people, like what happened in this example. It is surprising to note that there are some even to this day who are still nursing the idea that there should be some people today who should be slaves. Although the laws say there should be no slave trade, there are some who, if they are left unchecked, could go back to those slavery days. However, not all Anglicans were involved in something that is morally wrong (complicit). DR. Beilby Porteus the bishop of London was an evangelical was person who favoured everyone to be free, whenever he was preaching, he preached against slavery. Similarly, the Clapham sect, a group of Anglicans based around Clapham, South London carried out sterling work to end slave trade.

24

Faith and The Brain

We should take time to reflect on how we view God, this might have a beneficial effect on our brains. Spiritual practices have a beneficial and measurable effect on the brain, how does God change your brain? Like anything else, if you do it more often you will become addicted, the same applies with God's work the more you do it the more you will be used to it. Through research we find out that spiritual experiences shift perception, and can moderate the effects of stress on mental health. There is a decreased activation in the parts of the brain responsible for stress and increased activity in the parts of the brain responsible for connection with others. Prayer and spirituality have been linked to better health, greater psychological well-being, less depressions, less hypertension, less stress even during difficult times, more positive feelings, superior ability to handle stress. Religion activates the same giving you a good feeling of preparing something by a special method processes brain circuits as sex, drugs, and other addictive activities. A person's brain becomes more sensitised to the effect of carrying messages between nerve cells (serotonin), and molecule that plays several important rolls in cells (dopamine), which might help us to understand how retreat programmes of this nature can improve measures of wellbeing in this case, decreased self-reported tension and fatigue.

People who spend untold hours in prayer or meditation go dark in the parietal lobe, the brain area that helps create a sense of self. These people may be rewriting the neural connections in their brains –altering how they see the world. Staying in prayer is a way of staying in connected with divine. It is called neuroethology although it is new, it is drawing prominent researchers, scientists have found that a big number of people who spend untold hours in prayer and meditation are different. Examples of spirituality are: volunteerism, social responsibility.

How do we Measure Effects of Spirituality?

To meet the requirements of spirituality, you need to concentrate, and meditate on it. Spirituality is an important theme in health research, since a spiritual orientation can help people to cope with the consequences of serious disease. However, it needs divine intervention to be able to do exactly as is required.

The goodness of the power of prayer is that it will deliver us from the powers of darkness, and makes our relationship with God a good relationship. There are some hidden powers in prayer and meditation, this may sometimes lead to the intervention of divine powers, the level of spirituality cannot be measured, it will only depend on, normally when filled with the spirit you feel confident you will have self-control and self-esteem. This might help you to have a full life, and being able to think things out for yourself. To be good spiritually, you have to be a good listener and to be able to process what you have heard, this will help you to stay in the right direction. Whenever you hear of something look for the meaning and purpose, for everything happen or is done for a purpose. Staying in prayer will give you better health and psychological well-being, which may mean less depression and less hypertension, this is very helpful especially during difficult times, because like this you will be staying positive which gives you the ability to overcome stress. Spirituality and religious practices are a key part of many people's lives, 81% of the adults can claim to be spiritually filled. Some adults engage in some form of spiritual practice. it is not quite clear about what happens in certain parts of the brain during these spiritual experiences. Studies have linked specific brain measure to aspects of spirituality non have sort to directly examine spiritual experiences particularly when using a broader modern definition of spirituality that may be independent of religiousness.

Help to Preserve the Aging Brain

Long term meditation helps to preserve the aging brain than no meditators when they are aging. Scientists have found a relationship between relaxation and health, there is growing evidence that spiritual practices have a beneficial and can be measurable.

Always take care of your physical health, do some exercises these will strengthen the body and stay fit, and also heart health and will fight aging. You should closely watch meditation and see how it changes, improves your memory this will reduce stress and this will affect how you think and how you will behave. (Read the book,

How God Changes your Brain

Findings from a leading Neuroscientist: for your mental, physical, and spiritual health. Based on new evidence called from brain-scan studies, a wide-reaching survey of people's religious and spiritual experiences.

Taking a long time thinking of God and all the spiritual things or spiritual values, will change the structure of parts of the brain that controls our moods, give rise to our conscious notions of self and shape our sensory perception of the world.

The personality you assign to God has distinct neural patterns that collarette with your own emotions, styles of behaviour, how someone reacts at any one time. Reality scan shows that people who spend untold hour in prayer or meditation go dark in the parietal lobe located near the back and top of the head, the brain area that helps create a sense of self. A researcher says these people may be rewriting the neural connections in the brain- altering how they see the world: will see the world differently.

As long as you are in it, the brain will be able to easily engage in religious and spiritual practices. It does not matter whether you are praying in your head or you are praying aloud God hears all prayers, but if you are praying in your head be careful that you do not get disturbed and get detracted from your goals. People pray on bended knees opening their hearts to God, asking Him for so many different things; healing of cancer, a job after all these months, a buyer of their house in a frozen market, the end of pain, some prayers will be answered, the recipient will look heavenward with thankful praise.

God will answer your prayers, but that doesn't mean He will give you what you ask for, because He knows what is best for you. He will answer your prayers in His way. Try to ask for things that are in harmony with the will of God. This depends on what are the motives of your prayers, some prayers are driven by pride deep down our hearts, for God sees what is in our hearts, so let us be very careful in our prayers. If you knowingly condone a sin, if you remember of any wrong doing that you have done to God, confess it and repent, and face God with a clean heart, for He is righteous. Be honest on your prayers, learn to live what you pray for, for if you do not keep your promise, how will the Lord trust you? When you make promises to God learn to keep your promises, for if you break them how will the Lord trust you.

God allows struggle and difficult times because we are sinners, and we all come short of the glory of God. God loves us, but because of our sinful nature, He allows these things to happen. God does not cause suffering, but He can, and may allow it to accomplish good. Through His inspired scriptures, we learn that God will always answer our prayers, and will answer them if we address Him with faith and real intent. In our hearts we will feel the confirmation that He does hear us, this gives us a feeling of peace and calm. We can also feel that everything will be fine when we follow the father's will.

Our ways are not God's ways, sometimes we might feel we are not answered, while we do not know that He answers in His own ways, because He makes His plans well ahead of time, but we just want to see things happening there and then. Do not be shaky in your prayers, know what you are asking for and be firm, clarify what you want and tell God, this shows how faithful you are in your prayers. When you are simple and straight forward, wait for the answer, be patient and know that He is God.

Humble yourself, because He is also humble, He gave an example of humility, God speaks to us in so many different ways. It is up to us to know that He is speaking to us, otherwise we miss His call to us. Jesus, however, calls us to live within the environment of God's rule. We should always be seeking and searching for God with each breath we take and each moment that passes. Living in the (Kairos) of God carries with it an emphasis of being in the present. Every time we have to acknowledge God as God giving Him all the glory to lead us and keep us in the right path.

According to the Bible, there are "three heavens." The first one is our atmosphere, the second one is where the stars and planets are, and the third, where God dwells. The Bible also says God is omnipresent.

You can talk to God aloud or inside your mind, which ever feels most effective to you. It may be best to find a quiet or private space you can occupy in order to concentrate while you are talking. There may be a right or a wrong way of praying. When you pray, you pray for the things that are beyond you or your abilities. You can pray to thank God for the things He has granted you. When it comes to things to do with others, God sends you into a mission impossible. There are signs that God is answering prayers. We can know through the scriptures, because God mostly through His word. Sometimes you see that your desires are met, or sometimes by seeing the environment.

Sometimes we want God to do what we want, and we start saying that your prayers are not answered. (John 18:36) (NIV) It may be that we want heavenly things to be turned into earthly things, which makes it very impossible to such prayers to answered, because His kingdom is not of this world. If we know Him better, we to be glad when He says know to our request because sometimes it is for our good.

(1 Kings 19:12) (NIV) God at times speaks to us in a small still voice, like when He spoke to prophet Samuel when he heard His voice. (1 Samuel 3) (NIV) Most of the time God's voice sounds ordinary, that is the reason why most of us will miss His call because it sounds ordinary that you cannot even think it is God calling you. Let us do both listening and watching while He speaks to us, because we might miss Him, and it will be difficult to get that opportunity again.

When we pray, we are asking God to be involved in our ways or us to be involved in His ways, whichever is possible. "How to live for Jesus" Spend time praying each day, serve others, study the Bible, share God's word with other people, resist temptations, put God first, do not too much value in material things, trust God's plan. Always try to recognise God when He communicates with you. (Isaiah 43:18-19) (NIV) "Forget the former things; do not dwell on the past."

25

Kingdom Variance

What Happens After Death?

After death, the soul lives, the Lord looks after the soul in a place only known by Him alone and His angels. The reason why God inspired scriptures to be made because that is what He wants His people to know things that He knew we would meet in our walk of life even the things we meet in our social life are there so when we see them, we must know that they are there for a purpose. God knows that He created His people differently, with different feelings, what can move you, someone will not be moved. So, the writers of the Bible did not write what they wanted but what they were inspired to write. Whatever you see in the scripture, know that it was done for your good and for them to lead you to eternal life. The Lord wants us to follow what is in the scriptures because He inspired them to be written, if we follow their instruction, we will be saved. To obey these scriptures will make us perfect and make us furnished and make us pure and perfect people of God. The Bible promises us that there is life after death, if there was no life after death, He would not have to send His Son into the world so that no one should perish, (Psalms 23:4) (NIV) The verse says we can pass through that valley without any fear because we are promised that He is with us all the time. Death is very dreadful yes, but he says I will fear no evil. (John

11:11-14) (NIV) that is the reason why He inspired all scriptures to be written in order for us to prepare for that future life. This verse has demonstrated that Jesus has power over death, and this shown that we will also rise from death if we follow Him. (Revelations 21:4) (NIV) The Lord promises us new things, He promises to wipe away all tears, that is, when He makes everything new. Let us visualise what eternity will be like, that will be the happiest moment because there will be no going back to the times that were corrupted by the devil, like the time we are living in now. (Psalms 23:4) (NIV) When death comes no one will escape it, we struggle to try to avert it, but we are unable to, there is pain and there is crying because death is painful. Words of comfort are that there is one who walks with us in that fearful valley taking us to where there is no pain, but there is eternity, there is a shepherd who is shepherding our souls, He is the only one who will take us to eternity. We are now told that those pains caused by the devil are only temporal, our saviour provides us with all the protection we need to see us through. Our central message is that God always provide and protects, because of His love to us. (Ecclesiastes 9:5) (NIV) This encourages us to be cheerful in God regardless of what is happening in our lives todays. Although the writer of Ecclesiastes looks at life as vanity, this time is optimistic that there is some goodness after death, what a relief! People of the Old Testament were uncertain about the life after death but with the resurrection of Christ it is quite certain now that we are following Jesus' footsteps, and having faith in Him the resurrection of our souls is certain and assured, Jesus suffered for us. This life will not be a life of bones and flesh, it will be a spiritual life, this life is not automatic to everyone, but to those who will have followed the guide lines. He laid the guidelines in the scriptures, which should be followed by those who would like to prepare for that life. The good news is that it is free to everyone who wishes, the requirement is only obedience to the guidelines. God did not hide this, but He put everything clearly in the Bible for everyone to read for themselves. For those who cannot read he sends interpreters of the Bible whom He calls preachers who can explain step by step the requirements of the scriptures. No one might have an excuse for not knowing the requirements for preparing one's self for that life after death. So, he gives everyone a chance to prepare for that life to come, which no one will be taken unawares.

The Rich Man and Lazarus?

(Luke 16:19-31), the Pharisees thought that wealth was proof of a person's righteousness. Even today we tend to be carried away and going in the same direction as the Pharisees went, we have to ask to be filled with the Spirit of the Lord and to be able to walk in the right direction. Jesus disproved them by telling this story and giving them its meaning. The rich man did not go to hell because of his wealth, but because of his selfishness, (a very good lesson indeed). The amount of money we have is not as important as what we use it for. How do you use your money, do you hoard it selfishly or you use it to help others? This Lazarus should not be confused with the Lazarus who was raised by Jesus in John chapter 11 they are quite different. Sometimes we fail to get some advice looking down upon who had brought the message, Jesus told the rich man that they must listen to those who are preaching to them no matter who they are and not them expecting someone to come from the dead, even Jesus Himself, after his resurrection some still do not believe Him, so there is no point in bringing any one from the dead, still they will not believe him. Let us swallow our pride and start listening to whoever brings the word, the Lord has done His part, let us do ours. It is believed that the main point of this parable is to warn the godless wealthy about their need for repentance in this life, and Jesus did not intend to give a preview of life after death. It teaches in this particular case that both identity and memory remain after death for the soul of one in a hell. The message here is that worldly and earthly possessions are of no benefit they are not to be relied upon they are of no use in the afterlife. Those who have suffered on earth will receive their reward in heaven. At the resurrection, Jesus demonstrated that our souls will rise again and there is life after death. God has power over life, death, and resurrection, no one else has got the power, ours is to put our faith in Him alone. We appear to be doing the opposite when God says, racism has no place in charity, because in charity we have to love everyone.

We should help others regardless of where they come from or what they believe in. We are created equal, no one race is superior to the other or inferior from the other. At the end of the day, we belong to the same race humanity.

When they teach about the rich to be careful, they do not say wealth is bad, but only that we may get carried away if we are not careful, like anything else, we can get addicted in wealth in such a w ay that we may forget that we are not here for ever. There should be a good example that no one has been here for ever we are all going one by one. We came with nothing we will go with nothing, so there is no point in bragging about wealth and forgetting to work for our souls. The kingdom of heaven is very tricky because no wealth is required there, but only here on earth where moth and rust and thieves are. The raising of Lazarus from the dead made the Pharisees to hate Jesus even more. The raising of Lazarus made the disciples to know that Jesus was the saviour and the Messiah.

26

The Difference Between the Kingdom of God and the Kingdom of Heaven

The first thing Jesus preached about was the kingdom of God. This kingdom is meant to be a Spiritual kingdom and is a spiritual reality. The kingdom of God is the realm in which God reigns supreme and in complete sovereign, He is in control and in authority.

God is Holy and righteous; His Holy behaviour is the behaviour that accords with that infinite worthy and beauty. This overlaps with being morally right (righteousness) and unwavering pledges to look after us (commitment). 1 Peter 1:13-25) (NIV) So, if we want to be like Him, we have to live a life of holiness and faithfulness full of goodness and always giving glory to God. Always giving attention to matters of righteousness and self-disciplined life. A life of justice and a life of service to other people and a life of selflessness. We must stop putting our energy on perishable things but to put our trust and faith on Him who bought us not with perishable silver or gold but precious blood that will never lose its power

Jesus brought us the new covenant that is written in our hearts, Jesus intercedes between us and God. The new covenant that was brought by Jesus should be written in our hearts not on a piece of stone as in the time of Moses. The difference with the old and new covenant is that you have to give yourself to Jesus who will transform your life inside out.

The devil is still desperate to lead people astray by pretending to bring some new ideas for leading people away from the truth of the Lord. (Genesis 3:15) (NIV) Even though the devil tries to deceive us and tries to lead us astray, through his lies, we have salvation from Jesus Christ, who on His resurrection defeated the devil. This means the head of the snake was crushed as promised that the son of a woman would crush the head of the snake, already on that day our salvation plan was laid out showing that the striking of the heel is not as deadly as the crushing of the head of the snake. The writer is pleading with the reader not to be led astray by the lies of the devil whose head was crushed out at the resurrection. (Ephesians 6:12) (NIV) The resurrection assured us of salvation, but the salvation does not come in a plate, because there are forces of darkness which are trying to mislead us into believing that you will get something from the devil. We have to keep watch so that we do not fall into the devil's trap.

(Hebrews 12:14) When you do whatever you do you must know that you are doing it for the Lord, not to please any earthly people, but for the Lord who sees everything, even those things that are in our hearts. For us to stay pure we must strive always to do good: strive to have peace with everyone: strive always to stay holy for that is what the Lord wants us to be always: we must be in pursuit of the holiness: his moral laws will lead us to holiness which is what the Lord requires of us. To be holy, always confess your sins and always try to be good to everyone. Have total commitment to the Lord who bought us not with perishable silver or perishable gold, but with precious blood which never loses value. (1 Peter 1:14-16) There are so many forces which want to lead us astray, but as sons and daughters of the living God we have to stay alert waiting for his coming, we must stay focused and always on the alert. His laws are for us to keep our morality which is good for us in the end, if we keep his laws, that means we will be like him and stay as pure as he is and become members of his family. That family is not a corrupted family, stays pure, is not blood thirsty not war like but full of love always. No matter how much you commit yourself to Christ, you will always get temptations and those forces which want to pull you back. It is not easy to achieve this but to be always committed to God, always trying to keep yourself apart from the sins of this world. The Lord will do His part to help you to overcome these trials and temptations.

Distinction of the Kingdoms

People must see from our deeds that we are representing the kingdom of God here on earth, that means the kingdom will be revealed through us. When Jesus said the kingdom has come, He meant that after His stay on earth where he would be teaching about the kingdom, He would leave us with the Holy Spirit who would be with us all the time of our lives. So, the kingdom would always be with us, so we would not be comfortless. When Jesus said the kingdom of God is within you, He meant that we will always have someone to guide us. The three gospels were using the words "kingdom of God" and "kingdom of heaven" inter changeably, Mark and Luke referred to it as the "kingdom of God" while Matthew referred to it as the "kingdom of heaven" because Matthew was writing to the Jews mainly, who were very strict in using the name "God "Jesus want us to know that there are some sins we would want to grade ourselves and say these are minor sins, those will affect us great and make us to be the least in the kingdom of heaven, we must regard every sin as sin.

Change your thinking about yourself and about God, and start regarding every thought about God as you are talking to God start believing that God dwells in you and do not forget that this promise was given to us, and the one who promised it does not promise lies. (Psalms 46:10) "Be still and know that I am God: I will be exalted among the nations: I will be exalted in the earth". We have to reflect on the great works that He has done, that will remind us to give all the glory to Him.

One unforgivable sin is blasphemy against the Holy Spirit (Mark 3:28-30) (NIV) Do use the name of God in vain, such as when you exclaim, or something pressing. Where you think that you have fended God, confess and repent other than giving it off until some other time.

The Fulfilment of the Heavenly Kingdom on Earth

Jesus likened the kingdom of God to a mastered seed which is smaller than other grain seeds but grows in to a very huge tree, so Jesus was saying our faith should be likened unto a mastered seed. The kingdom of God is also known as the kingdom of heaven. In Christianity the spiritual realm is where God reigns as king, it is also the fulfilment on earth of God's will. The kingdom of God has broken into history this has worked through the Holy Spirit whom He uses through the church. The church is here to represent the kingdom of God or the kingdom of heaven, when accepted in people's hearts, then the kingdom of heaven is on earth. The mission of the church is to accomplish the will of God on earth, the coming reign of God is the coming of love peace and justice. The death and resurrection of Jesus was the beginning of the fulfilment of this. This must continue until the time of the judgement when this will be fully established on earth. Jesus explained fully His mission on earth in (Luke 4:18) (NIV) Jesus claimed that He had come to set free the oppressed to give freedom to all prisoners of sin, He called it the year of Jubilee to all slaves He has got to recover sight to all those who are spiritually blind Sometimes we misrepresent His mission on earth and start expecting Him to be a political leader. When we are oppressed, we tend to want Him to quicken our liberation which most of the time ends in our disappointment. We must always ask Him to liberate us spiritually because that will give us eternal freedom. The fruits and values of the kingdom of God are: faith to His promise to stay pure in heart and in deeds, to feel to be like those who are suffering and the oppressed not for us to be oppressing them, loving God and loving your neighbour, be honest and truthful in whatever you do humility and to have joy in other people's achievements, wealth and ambitions must not give us pride.

(Matthew 19:23-24) (NIV) Jesus told His disciples how hard it was for someone who was rich to enter the kingdom of heaven. And how easy it was for a camel to go through the eye of a needle than for someone who was rich to enter the kingdom of God. In the same verse Jesus has used the two words freely the kingdom of heaven and the kingdom of God

Jesus was exemplary

The kingdom of God is a righteousness, and joy in the Holy Spirit, this kingdom only comes through repentance and living a pure life that pleases God. When Jesus lived this life on earth, He was giving an example of how we would live our lives. Some theories say kingdom of God and kingdom of heaven are the same thing. We find the best example in (Matthew 19:23-24) (NIV) Jesus was warning us that we had to be very careful that with wealth we could easily be carried away without knowing that we are carried away. Jesus was saying to them it was impossible to try to enter the kingdom using flesh and blood. However, He did not leave them like that, but He explained to them that with God everything was possible, meaning that spiritually it was possible, He even made it clear that since God is spirit, we should worship Him in truth and in Spirit. He was making it clear to us that we have to look after the poor for His eyes are on the poor, be good to them because some of them did not choose to be what they are, He said He came for the poor and the oppressed. Being rich is not something that started yesterday, it was there long ago and there were some rich men who made it to heaven. Money is not the root of evil, but love of money is the root of evil, because if you love it more than your God then it becomes evil, let us have some awareness and use our wealth as God wishes and let us keep our relationship with Him. Likewise, the apostles Luke and Mark use kingdom of God while Matthew uses kingdom of heaven when they wrote about exactly the same parable. So, it appears the two phrases are interchangeable.

27

All future Generations of the People: (Posterity)

Our generation is trying the best they can so that the next generation will inherit something that will make them have good foundation on which to build their own and also leave something for the generation that will come after them. We must not lose focus that we also inherited something from our forefathers so the next generation must inherit something from us, so we must try by all means to record some of the things we do for the future generation (posterity). All future generations of people: example: there is an accident, the names of the victims have to recorded for reference with the coming generation (posterity). The decedents of a person: God offered Abraham a posterity that is, he was told that his off springs would be as uncountable as the stars of heaven. Sometimes it means those who come after us this includes our children and grandchildren.

Have an Interesting Destiny Ahead of me

To realise a destine ahead of you, is to keep on striving for the betterment of those goals. We have to keep on striving for our lives to be better, it is not easy but we to keep on striving. In life, what you do try to do it to the best of your ability, that is, doing things willingly, not neglecting whatever you do.

"Keep your best wishes, whatever you do you must have a commitment, keep everything close to your heartland, watch what happens. Do not set your goals by what other what is important to others is not what is important to you people deem important. Do not think of doing bad to other people as this will not improve your weaknesses. It is a sign of good breeding to appreciate what others do, give them a credit to what they have done good. If you always strive to do good, it means you are always striving for the best, which sometimes pays handsomely. Sometimes the failures that happened to us before in our lives before will hold us back, yet we should confess and move on, because the future is holding something good for us. Let us concentrate on the things that we value in life; they will help us to keep our life at a high standard of living. Please pick yourself up no matter how long the failure has taken, because that courage will build you up. There will always be failures in our lives, but is better that they should make you think and give you courage to do good and succeed in future. Do not allow failure to play with your brains, because that is the biggest weapon of failure. The best way forward in life is to try to avoid some mistake, they can be avoided by keeping vigilant all the time. The best way forward is to forget the past and look ahead to a bright future, which you can always achieve if there is a will. Let those failures be bridges to build your successful future and repentance. It is very hard to achieve anything if you doubt yourself, motivation gives us the desire to succeed. If you cannot motivate yourself, who is going to motivate you: always strive to make dreams come true, and start making life easy. Always work towards fulfilling your dreams or answering your call. The calls usually come in a very silent way, watch out for them they may pass you without noticing them. With will power, what you want to achieve in life is attainable, once you have that determination, you are moving towards your goals, it is always good to remember that good things are yet to come, so look forward to the good things, that is positive thinking. Be always looking forward to happy days ahead, always believe it will happen and it does. You must always have a firm determination; many things may be possible if you have the zeal to do them. Most of the time in life, if you are like that nothing will stand in your way, you will always have your way. Once you achieve that, you will know that these things are achievable, then they are at your fingertips, you start aiming higher. When you remember the failures in your life, you should correct them because they are doing no good to your life, hence you are making your future better. If you do not doubt yourself, that will give you confidence in doing bigger things in life, that paves the way for your progress in life. Motivate yourself because this is the way to give yourself confidence to do bigger and better things in your way to a sound living. It is very rare for other people to motivate you because they have their own problems also. In most cases if you motivate yourself that means you will be doing the things you are supposed to be doing, which is the way to make an achievement. In most cases in life, we are failing to answer a call not that we do not want to, but that we are not taking it seriously as in most cases we may not know it is a call. Everyone wants to achieve their goals, so what has been said is the best way to achieve, those goals. Let us all keep on aiming higher, for always aiming higher will build our humanity.

Your Present and Your Future Life

If you make good the present, that means the future will shape itself, strive by all means to ensure the present is good, there is no way the future will be bad, because it will be following in the footsteps of goodness. Be mindful of the present in order to shape your future, stop living in the past. You may cast your eyes to the past but do not dwell there. It is better to start shaping your future as you see the present, instead you should be leaving the past as something gone, people keep on worrying about the past. Instead, people should use the past and the present to build their future on that. The future is what we long for because we are all looking for a brighter future. Especially the future of eternal life is what we should strive for. Value your eternity and start working towards that life. We should learn to value our future legitimate desires that is when we can acquire a true sense of worth. The environment can influence people's behaviour and motivation to act in the way you do. The environment can influence mood, for example, rooms with bright lights, both natural and artificial, can improve health outcomes such as depression agitation and sleep. Too much deforestation may cause siltation which may result into desert and cause climate change. So, people have to be educated of the dangers of not taking care of the environment. In life we face so many challenges, sometimes it is because of the environment we were raised up in. As we grew up in this corrupt world, that means we were defiled one way or another, which means that we were contaminated polluted or tainted, this means we were made impure or unclean, yet we were meant to be pure before God. This may also mean our image was violated to the extent that means we are no more worth what we were supposed to be. We should try to create inner peace by making ourselves or choose not to allow other people or events to control your anger, you yourself must learn to control your anger and also control your emotions, let us understand our own inner world, so we have to strive to purify ourselves so as to have a brighter future. We should have a desire to correct our future, you have to change your habits this will change your future and change your life for the better. It is true that we have desires to achieve specific goals but sometimes we fail to achieve them. Remember, procrastination will not achieve any goals but to draw you back in life. By reflecting on the past, they will help us to correct and move on for a bright future is all what we aim for. Do not feel defeated and despair, once fell to the ground, stand up and continue the race you will win the race of life. Sometimes these mis harps want to pin us to the ground arise and continue. Find where you did wrong, correct it fast and continue so that you forget about those wrongs and continue. After reflecting on the past, when we see the wrongs, we have done, considering that I want a better present and a better future, these must strengthen my feelings. When reflecting on the past, you will always find where you did not do well, you might have hurt others, apologise even if you cannot see them anymore. This might hound you and slow down your progress in life, the best way to free yourself is to make an apology to whoever you hurt and ask for forgiveness, and free yourself for the sake of progress in your future. Do not let the past hold you at ransom, be prepared to forgive or apologise in order to forget about the past. Do not keep someone a prisoner because they wronged you, do not make other people do what you want by using threats because you have not done anything about it. It is you who can change your future, and change who you are, you can change your future for the better by wanting to correct what you did wrong in the past.

What I was Born for

God created us for a purpose as long as we live we must be useful to other people help to develop the world by your labour your skills your advice to others, if they are realised to their potential they will be useful to the world.

Birth started at creation, although the first man was created, the subsequent man was born. Primarily, God created man to represent the heavenly kingdom on earth that is why the word says man was given dominion over everything on earth, it was for a purpose to represent the kingdom, that means a man has to do the will of God on earth. The Christian lifestyle must show that we really mean representing the kingdom of heaven. We need to ask God to help us to understand His kingdom, because without the guidance of the Holy Spirit we may think that we understand it but really, we do not understand it. As God is eternal, so His kingdom is eternal, God's kingdom goes beyond the limit of (Transends) time and space, so it is good for us to seek this kingdom first. A man has got to go through the experience of life, which has got ups and downs. As man had gone through physical creation, God also put a soul in man which is the spiritual part of creation or being born. The is distinct from the physical part of creation it is the spiritual part of creation.

Born means being brought to life by a process of being formed in a woman's womb and brought out at birth, not creation. Your age is determined from the date of birth onwards. When you are born, you cry, and the world rejoices. Live so that when you die, you rejoice, and the world cries. That they lough when you are gone. Living in the present allows you to build a whole world that will then become your legacy. Living in the present implies being aware of each situation and finding our eternity in every single moment. When people lack experience or wisdom, they spend time blaming the environment as being bad without them putting the environment into good use. They will spend their time looking at other places while standing on an island their surrounding is full of life opportunities.

In most cases, the way you act now will affect your future, so be very careful of today. It is true that your current life is, to a large extent, the result of your past actions, choices and experiences. The great news, however, is that your future is determined by how you act in the present moment. Your past is there to remind you of the wrongs you did, so as not to repeat them in the future. If your past reminds you of something good you did in the past, it reminds you to keep it up or to improve on it and do better. Your future is determined by your present. In the past I wasted precious time which will never be recovered, I did not take care of my health as was required, I always wish those wasted opportunities could be returned to me, I would do better to make my future life worth living.

What is The Purpose of Life?

God created us for a purpose, we must not lose focus and start thinking that you have no purpose. Sometimes we have everything we want but still feel empty, if you feel satisfied with what you have, is a good sign for thanking the Lord with what you are or with what you have. There must be a difference between thanking God and boasting, for it is not by our works but by faith, for whatever we succeed in our lives we have to be thankful from the bottom of our hearts knowing that it is by His grace. This does not mean that we should stop working because we have enough, we are saying that we should stop being greedy, but to have enough to be able to help others for the good of the Lord. We are expected to work for the Lord while we are still on earth, at the same time working for eternity. The other thing that might stop us from knowing what we are or who we are is that we may not have done research of our lives and discover what potential we might have. Sometimes we have some hidden strength in us, actually people should live their real life. In our lives, there are some fears that are planted by the devil, so that you keep on thinking that you are too inferior for that, look at your life and break the barriers set up to block you from progressing in your life. Why are you not there yet? Is because there is a barrier set up to block you from making it in life, there are some unique geniuses in you, there is something worthwhile in you. Study yourself and be clear in what you want, find something that suits you. You have a talent that others do not have, why not pursue it, here now, it is you who knows how you can approach your goal. Find satisfaction when your goals start unfolding, feel comforted and feel that there are some powers enabling you to achieve that. Your beliefs your thoughts of empowering yourself will help you to overcome some of this inferiority complex in your life and start progressing in your life. Build some relationship with those powers that enable you, always ask to walk the spiritual path of your life. Your spiritual journey is something that is very personal to yourself, regardless of what you believe in when it comes to everything else in life. For many, following a spiritual path is like searching for something that makes them complete. What is it that you truly want to do? Strive to achieve what you can, professionally or personally, all that are your values in life, those values really matter in your life. There are some gaps in your life, bridge them for your progress. The most draw back in our lives is that we procrastinate to implement or address some of those issues in life.

Sometime in life, we get to be comfortable and forget that you must not find comfort in life without trying to explore something new, and start your spiritual journey in your life you need something to insight your heart and start burning. If we look closely, we see that there is some void space in your soul which needs filling. With some of these things we need guidance because sometimes on our own we cannot fill them. When we are told to discipline ourselves, it will appear like the rules are hash, but only that they are meant to make us fit. Let us always strive to realise our calling in life. Go on a spiritual journey and fulfil your desires.

Sometimes we comfort ourselves that I have done very well in life therefore that is enough yet there is still a lot that you need to accomplish in life. We are used to saying I am better than them, so I must sit back and relax. There are still so many learning opportunities to learn out there.

The Spiritual Journey of Life

"A spiritual journey is a journey you would take to find out who you are, what your problems are in life, and how to come to peace with the world. The purpose of a spiritual journey is rarely to find an answer; rather, it is a process of continually asking questions. If it is targeted for the general public will not tell you what your spiritual movement should look like should look like, but will give you tools that you may find important in doing it according to plan of your journey.

Understand that you journey is yours alone

This is because every person is unique, because the problems faced by each individual are different, and the way each responds to them differs according to each individual. Although we may get some advice from others, they may be general, it is a generalised advice because they do not know exactly how it affects you. It is for you to put the ideas together and with your own ideas and see if they add up when you put them together with your own solutions. That means when you get an advice, you had your own way of thinking, as long as you can see that it may help your situation, then you implement it which means it is now your baby. That means it was you who was satisfied the it would work for you, then that it is your responsibility, that means you have found a way that will not harm you. Have a wide range of consultation before you start implementing your ideas because they will affect your life, and no one else's life.

Keep a journey of your thoughts and feelings

Whatever you do it must be thoughtful because you are already on your journey of life. Analyse your feelings, fears, thoughts and your expectations what you do in a day or what you do in many days, weeks, months or years, study yourself so that you understand yourself. If you study yourself, that means you will know your weaknesses and your strengths, that means you are taking a well-planned journey of your life.

Make a set of goals and prioritise them

In life organised things are a joy of life, when things are organised, they tend to make life easy they will also help to organise something in future, think and stay calmer and always control your anger. If you do not control your anger, it retards your progress in life. A well-planned journey will help you to heal whatever might want to come in your way. The spiritual journey helps to live a healthier life, do not allow your goals to stress you.

Decide on the scope of your journey

Spiritual journeys are long life affairs, they build upon themselves it interesting to know that it is a crucial part of life, you cannot fragment them but to keep them together as one family.

Your Ultimate Destiny

It is better to look at life and see that you are made to live for a purpose. It is better to look at life broadly, then you can discover that the Lord keeps you for a purpose. In most cases we under rate ourselves. Let us remember that whatever we are doing, we are working for the Lord, so let us do it to the best of our ability. The Bible reveals your future and purpose for existing. Holy scripture shows why God created mankind. Learn why you were born and how to join God's family. Ask, why were you born? what is the purpose of life, can you have an interesting and fulfilling destiny ahead of you, regardless of your present situation? We expect to live a spiritual life after this life, that is eternity.

There is Life Beyond Death

It is interesting to note that there will be life after death but that we will not be in the physical body as we are in now. We have souls, so that will resurrect. Since it is pointed out that it is not all who will resurrect but the saints only. So, it is difficult in this life to tell who is the saint and who is not. The advice is to have faith and only believe. It is very reliving and strengthening to realise that we find everything in Christ even beyond this life. When we are faced with death of loved ones, we tend to get confused and forget that death comes in turns, our turn is also on the way, the only solution is to start preparing for it now. When you are prepared for it, you will fear nothing even death. There must be something we value the most in our lives, we must value life very much. This is the time to talk to God, and start amending where you find you did not go well with God, that is if you have sinned against His will. When you realise what you have done, confess and repent, spend time with God for that is the best way to have good relationship with Him.

28

What is the Proper Place of the Church?

A church is central to the Christian faith, and it is where the community comes together to worship and praise God, a place of worship for all Christians, where the work of charity is carried out. The church plays a vital role in helping Christians and non-Christians by providing help to those who are suffering, the helpless and the homeless. It provides them with food or with shelter, which means it is following in the footsteps of Jesus Christ whose mission on earth was specifically for the poor and the helpless. Jesus said, even if He was gone, the poor and the needy will still be with you. (Matthew 25:35-36) (NIV) The Holy Spirit gives us understanding on the word of God, so we have to rely on it. It is good news to understand that it teaches us of the heavenly things and makes us understand them. He reminds us that there will be a judgement day when everything will be made clear, besides making these things clear to us, He prepares us to be ready for that day. Sometimes we want the heaven to do like we want, yet heaven never changes it is us who have to do what is done in heaven, included to what the Holy Spirit tells us, the Lord reveals heavenly things in scriptures. (Hebrews 10:24-25) (NIV) the church encourages believers to love one another and to be of service to one another, the believers also know that they are joined together by the blood of Jesus, so they consider themselves to be one family. They consider themselves as a group of people or a community of believers who encourage one another to stay pure always. Including meeting and worshipping, they say every member is a preacher in that their works must always show and reflect Christ, and be an example to others.

Governing authorities like the church, help the world to stay in peace. By having faith in Christ, then that has to be demonstrated to people by your deeds, that is, some people might emulate your good deeds then you have preached to them that way. Obedience is one of the disciplines of the Christianity, Jesus taught obedience even He Himself was obedient to His Father. So, when Christians are being asked to be obedient, they are not being asked to do something that He did not do, or to do the impossible. Effective listening is one of the qualities of a preacher and service to the people is one of the qualities of a preacher. The church community encourages each other to be friendly, what the church does should impact the community, and they encourage each other for good behaviour and to be very human, loving one another, and to be tolerant. When they say one another, they mean that everyone is created in the image of God, hence we are all brothers and sisters. The reason why they behave like that and encourage each other to be like that is that they take it from the words of Jesus where He says where two meet in my name I am there. They feel that Jesus is always there where they are at any time since He promised to be with us always.

The Holy Spirit Dwells in us

(Matthew 18.20) And also His promise that He would not leave us comfortless and that He would send us the comforter who will be with us all the days of our life. (John 14:18) (NIV) He asked us to be still and know that He is with us be still He said, and that He would not leave us as orphans or the comfortless, I will not leave you as orphans, meaning that God will not abandon when you face tribulations. Even when there is no hope, Jesus will never leave nor forsake us. The Lord Himself goes before you and will be with you: He will never leave you nor forsake you. Do not be afraid do not be discouraged. No one will be able to stand against you all the days of your life. As He was with those of old days, He will be with us will never leave us or forsake us. Therefore, where ever we are, whatever we are doing we must always bear in mind that He is there with us. Sometimes we tend to cheat ourselves because we think that no one is seeing us. This community of believers is very strict and wants to build a very closer relationship. They focus on being very polite to each other, both in deeds and manners. Jesus carried His mission in both deeds and words, do also to others as you have copied from Him you will be doing like Christ so you will be a true Christian as followers of Christ, our mission is to disciples who make disciples. The church is expected to do their things in one accord and fulfil the mission of Christ because when He knew He was going, He commissioned us to carry on where He left off. Since we are committed as His disciples, our task is to teach others we grow in our faith and come to Him in one accord. The story of the Bible is the story of God making His rule which has been hidden since because they are baked up by the authority of the government. The state is responsible to recognise and protect the church and the church is responsible to recognise and advise the state. Many consider it desirable that this material relationship between church and state should be clearly engrossed in the state's articles of Constitution. The church leaders have the responsibility to land their voices to the issue s of corruption injustice, impurity and other ill in the land. It is the responsibility of every Christian to proclaim the righteous ness of God in the land, particularly those whose voices can be heard. The church can play a vital role in assisting Christians to help others by providing food banks. Places where people living in poverty can go and collect food, help for the homeless. Housing justice is a Christian a Christian

Charity that tries to ensure everyone has a home. The three key foundations for nation building are: family, faith and education, without these three, it is practically impossible for any country to attain First World status and it is through these three that First World nations sustain their status. Christianity was committed to uphold social justice, equality and welfare of which helped a country to attain national development. The purpose of enumerating the contribution of Christianity was to correct the bad impression which the social critics might have generated. Nation building is the process whereby society of people with diverse origins histories, languages cultures and religions come together within the boundaries of a sovereign state with unified constitutional and legal dispensation, a national public education system, an integrated national economy, share symbols. The church exists primarily to proclaim the word of God that is so desperately needed by everyone still living, the church also exists to provide men the opportunity for fellowship with other believers. The first social teachings proclaim the respect for human life, one of the first fundamental needs in a world distorted by greed and selfishness. The church teaches that all human life is sacred and that the dignity of human person is the foundation of all the social teachings. The church, in whatever form it takes, is there to instruct society, the church's role in our world is to be the voice of God's truth to the modern world, not really to be involved in politics but to advise in order for society to stay on track. God used Moses to lead the children of Israel out of Egypt where they were under slavery, and bring them to Mount Sinai where God gave them a set of laws. These laws formed the basis for a new government. That government was theocracy. In other words, religion ran the government, and the laws were based on loyalty to the God of Israel. One Bible principle not mentioned by the What would Jesus cut activists is, you should not steal, (Exodus 20:15) NIV) Whatever government takes should be used for the common good, which means spending responsibly for a public purpose. The Church has to pray for our leaders (1 Timothy

2:1-4) (NIN) gives us direct instruction, our leaders need God's help. Religion can contribute to national integration, political mobilisation, reformation of ethnic identity. Nationalism, peaceful coexistence, economic, social and political development. The church's development introduced to the world the idea of human rights formalised and insisted upon due process decreed concern as necessary for marriage required criminal intent as intent of criminal responsibility, and popularised the idea of equality and justice as central to law and authority. Christianity has been intricately intertwined with the history and formation of Western Society. Throughout its long history the church has been major source of social services like schooling and medical care, an inspiration for art culture and philosophy. And an influential player in politics and religion. Nation-building aim at the unification of the people within the state so that it remains politically stable and viable in the long run. The government recognises the role of youth in nation building since these teenagers become the future leaders of the next generation The battle field of good governance and effective governance lies within the youth's ideals and principles today. The foundation of church social teachings should be inherent dignity of the human person as created in the image and likeness of God. The church therefore calls for integral human development, which concerns the wellbeing of each person in every dimension, economic, political ecological and spiritual. The Bible makes social justice a mandate of faith and a fundamental expression of Christian discipleship. From a scriptural point of view justice means loving our neighbour as we love ourselves and is rooted in the character and nature of God as God is just and loving, so we are called to do justice and live in love. The local church is responsible to serve one another in love equip saints for ministry, and to care for widows, orphans and those with physical needs. Additionally, the church worship collectively, reads and studies scriptures and protects the gospel and church from false teachers and deception. Research has shown that that people who regularly attend church report stronger social support networks and less depression. They lead healthier lives even longer lives. In a very real and physical way, church is literally good for your health. The church becomes the most important force in unifying society because the central government had become so weak. Christians believe that God made two areas of 9influencein the world-religious and political. (Romans 13:1-2) (NIV) Obey the government for God is the one who has put it there. So those who refuse to obey the law of the land are refusing to obey God. And punishment will follow. Citizens vote for leaders to represent them and their ideas, and the leaders support the interests of the citizens. There are two special rights only. Jesus told His listeners, to give to Caesar the things that were for Caesar, and to God the things that were God's (Matthew 22:21) (NIV) Jesus was clearly teaching obedience to Roman law and also to obey God's laws. It is for freedom that Christ has set us free. Stand firm then and do not let yourselves be burdened again by a yoke of slavery. Jesus once said whatever we do to the least of our neighbours, we do to Him, so if you really want to serve Him, the best Way to start is to serve the needy. You don't have to be Mother Theresa or Mahatma Gandhi. All of us are called to be servants of Christ in our own way. Governments should not cause inflation by overstepping of Biblical principles in economic policy. inflation encourages debt by deceives people about pay increases and future wealth accumulation. Families are religions and pull them towards greater self- consciousness needed to build and unmated a nation from within society is one of the most integral parts of our lives. Among various structures of life society too is one of the most under it. Their policy of being polite to each other should apply to everyone as well. As they meet regularly, they check on one another, what they do pays dividends in the end, because everyone will be well behaved, and keep themselves away from all works of being inhuman, and there is peace on earth. They always encourage each other to behave like that in the community, they think that by being exemplary, they may be attracting the community to emulate them so as to have a happy world to live in without laws being imposed on them. This will mean that, as we always ask for the heavenly kingdom to come, it will have come on earth. This community encourages each other to teach their children while they are still young, knowing that what is learnt at a young age will always stay. These young people are taught to say "please "or "thank you," some of these things which they are taught at a young age will be encoded in their DNA for the rest of their lives. What these people share, they expect every member to do it freely without anyone following them or anyone imposing them on anyone. Anyone who would like to go against these set rules will be politely shown the way in such a way that they feel like a fish out of the pond.

Christianity is There to Help Society

Christianity plays a very vital part in helping society because Christians do not want to see any one suffering so they provide things like food banks. They copy it from Jesus whose mission to earth was for the poor, so the church also sympathises with the poor. Christianity touches every part of our lives, Christianity has done a lot in alleviating human suffering, Christians are not politicians, but they appears like they are indulging into politics, yet it is only that they sympathise with the poor, not wanting to be political rulers, no, if it is looked at closely, the government could appreciate what Christians are doing because they teach society to behave and do it in a human manner, this reduces suicides reduces alcoholism and drug misuse which is good for the government because it would reduce crimes and have a civilised society. They do not want to see any one sleeping in the streets so they also provide housing for the poor, so the church tries to alleviate any suffering a human being might encounter. Jesus reminded us not neglect the poor for He came for that which we have to follow what He did and say, Jesus said, you have the poor with you always It is very important to be able to identify the poor and do not leave them like that because it is your responsibility, not the church or not the government, but the individual's responsibility.

The church must do this without looking at the colour of a person, for we are living in a multicultural society. The church can play a vital role in assisting Christians to help others by providing food banks. The church goes to places where people are living in poverty, and it collects some food for them. It also helps the homeless the homeless in the form of Housing Justice as a Christian Charity that tries to ensure everyone has a home. The cultural influence of Christianity includes social welfare, founding hospitals, economics as the protestant work ethic, natural law, which would later influence the creation of international law, politics architecture, literature, personal hygiene, and family life. Christianity affects the economy in such a way that, for given religious beliefs, increases church attendance tend to reduce economic growth. In contrast for given church attendance, increases in some religious beliefs—notably heaven, hell, and afterlife- tend to increase economic growth. The purpose of the church is to worship, fellowship, discipleship, ministry. And mission and that they derived from the great commandment; (Matthew 22:37-40) and the great commission (Matthew 28:19-20) The church also teaches about the "the preferential option for the poor" that in order to improve life for the poor, we should speak for the voiceless. Christians working in this movement focus on helping those who are in poverty. Followers of the Christian religion base their belief on the life, teachings and death of Jesus Christ. Christians believe in one God that created heaven earth and the universe. The belief in one God originated from the Jewish religion. Christians believe Jesus is the Messiah or saviour of the world. The Christians believe in prayer, and the coming together of believers called a church. They also believe in the baptism into the Christian church, whether this be as an infant, or as an adult, this is an outward sign of an inward commitment to the teaching of Jesus. Christianity is the faith tradition that focuses on the figure of Jesus

Christ, in this context faith refers both to the believers' act of trust and to the content of their faith. As a tradition Christianity is more than a system of religious belief.

Religion and social breakdown, the practice of religion has beneficial effects on behaviour and social relations. on encouraging couples to marry legally, and to do things that will cut down on crime rate. They are also found helping the people to abide by the laws, and to provide for those who are in need and dependency, alcohol, and drug abuse, suicide, depression and general self-esteem. As a consequence of political and economic stability of the society, they are embedded in, protestant radical sects perpetuate positive aspects of belonging to their religion; trust, lower divorce rates (marriage stability) education for the children, improved physical and mental health and higher levels of education. Church contributes a lot to the economy; they do much more than just provide places of worship.

29

The Kingdom of God Seeks to Control Lives from Inside Out

On earth, we must try to live a life that is devoted to doing the will of God, so as to be always pure and perfect and upright. If you let Christ rule in our lives, that is, let Him be in control, then that is the kingdom of God. (Matthew 6:33) (NIV) When we are saying, your kingdom come, we are inviting Him to come into our hearts, when we say this, we must really mean it, He is the one who knows everything even what we think. This brings us to (Luke 17:21) (NIV) where Jesus says, the kingdom is within you. (Romans 14:17) (NIV) All this means to surrender your life to Christ, when He uses you, it will make a difference in your life, please let your kingdom go away and replace it with His kingdom, be faithful, when you say it mean it. Something we must ask for His guidance that is, when we invite Him, we must not mix with our own thought which might mean we are divided, this does not bring the real kingdom, because He sees how much faith we have, before we say it to Him. This will teach us to follow His guidance, which means we may try to resist all types of sin or anything that might offend Him we keep away from them. That will mean ourselves trying to stay in His kingdom that is, if we stay clean there is no way He cannot stay in us, that is where our relationship with Him will be.

(Matthew 6:33) (NIV) Seeking first the kingdom of heaven before everything else, and everything will be added to you. In other words, the reality is, what you ask for, you will get. Seeking the kingdom is not like you are hunting the kingdom as if it were something tangible. It means you are seeking to be transformed, so that whatever you do the kingdom is manifested. The word of God guides us in our live that is, it becomes like a road map to our lives, because the work of the road map is to guide you until you reach your destination. So, the word is leading us to our destination which is eternal life. You are blessed if the kingdom of God is manifested on you, you are a letter that is read by the world. Your works and deeds are representing the heavenly kingdom, allow Him to use you inside out, He is more powerful, but the power sometimes comes late in life. Like Jesus did, He gave us an example, when He was led to the cross, His enemies under rated his power not knowing that He would resurrect on the third day. If you allow Him to rule in your heart, that means you will be like Him, which means the resurrection of your soul is assured. Let Christ rule in our lives, so His works will be seen when they manifest through our deeds. when it asks us to seek first the kingdom of God and His righteousness and everything will be added to us. When we respond to His word, we are saying God use us as you want us to be. We have no way we can have an excuse for not doing what is required of us because He came to be an example for us to follow. Whatever we can find as difficult, He went through it Himself.

The Temptation of Jesus by the Devil

(Luke 4:5-8) (NIV). When Jesus was targeted, He was alone in the desert, the devil might target us when we are alone. The word of God is our sword, faith in the word is our shield, we should seek riches and honours, and happiness in the worship of God. (Psalms 24:1) (NIV)

The earth is the Lord's and all that is in it, and all that it contains. By the lies of the devil, he claims it to be his, hence he attracts many to believe that they will benefit from them if they pay allegiance to the devil. God is the creator of the earth and, we have to have clean hands and a pure hearth in order to qualify for heaven, pull yourself away from things of vanity. We must always be on the alert by staying in prayer all the time reading the scriptures, thinking about God where ever you are so that you are not tempted, because the devil will always target us when we are alone, such as what he did to Eve when she was alone and to Jesus in the wilderness. You must always be thinking about the Lord when you are alone so that He stays near you so that you are never alone. The word of God is our sword, and faith in that word is our shield. God has many ways for providing for His people, and therefore is at all times to be depended upon in the way of duty. The ways of Satan are used as baits to snare us into big trouble all his promises are n deceitful, they are used to lead us to destruction. (John 18:36-37) (NIV) For now, who controls the kingdom of the world? Then the devil taking Him up on a high mountain, showed Him all the kingdoms of the world in a moment of time.

The devil is Still at work

And the devil said to Him. "All this authority I will give you and their glory: for this has been delivered to me and I will give them to whoever I wish. Therefore, if you worship before me, all will be yours" The devil said that wanting to lure Jesus into sinning, he can still say that to us today in order to take us away from God our Father. This shows us that we will always meet with some temptation, it is easy to do that as long as we are following Jesus' footsteps. And Jesus answered and said to him, "Get behind me Satan!", for it is written, "You shall worship the Lord your God, and Him only you shall serve" This will get us searching, who controls the worldly kingdom and its wealth. We have to ask for guidance on this because the devil might come to us with very attractive offers which sometimes, we may not be able to resist. Jesus was able to resist because He always stayed connected to His Father. The advice of the author is to remind us to stay connected, otherwise we will not be able to have the difference between a good offer or a bad offer. Since we are following the footsteps of Jesus Christ, we have to bear I mind that Jesus came to represent the heavenly kingdom, we must also represent the heavenly kingdom. To represent the heavenly kingdom means we have to be pure in our hearts. We must stop representing the heavenly kingdom by worldly methods, otherwise there is a very thin difference which requires spiritual eyes which we can only get if we stay connected above and below. When we ask for these powers let us remember not to mix the power with political power which seeks glory for one's self, or seeking prestige or building a name for myself and forgetting to promote what we are supposed to promote. Sometimes the kingdom of this world is got by using violent means to achieve it. If we earnestly seek His guidance, He can take us out of the kingdom of this world while we are still in this world. To be taken out of this world while you are still on this earth, require a lot of suffering and a lot of self-denial, giving your body as living and holy sacrifice for the sake of the heavenly kingdom. Be devoted and have complete obedience to God, to be for Him every step of your life. You will suffer humiliation when you want to promote meekness on this corrupt and harsh rule of this world. We must resist by all means to conform to this world. In this life means we will be struggling with the spirits of darkness, fighting against sin and the powers of Satan. (Ephesians 6:10-20) (NIV) We are fighting a spiritual warfare wedged by the devil, that is the biggest war in our lives, because we are fighting with unseen powers which sometimes becomes difficult to evade, because things may appear like they are in our favour, yet in the end they are the forces which are working against us. Jesus is really our saviour, when He knew that we were going to be faced with such, He sent to us the Holy Spirit who would dwell in us whatever we do and where ever we go, Holy Spirit is standing for us, that is why sometimes we win these wars without us knowing them. For us to be able to stand in front of the Lord, we must be separated from sin which is done by the Holy Spirit for us. As Christians we are urged to distance ourselves from unclean things so that we qualify to stay near the Lord who does not require unclean things near Him. There are some ungodly pleasures of the world which we must avoid, for if we are involved in them, they defile us. We should not love the world or anything that is in it, for if we love worldly things, we are distancing ourselves from our Father who is in heaven, after collecting worldly wealth we start boasting, and start looking down upon others. We cannot do two things at once following God and His love for good things, and the world with its pleasures, its lust and its corrupt ways of doing things does not please God who is righteous. If we are given worldly wealth by the Lord to help us survive, are we not ending up misusing them, ending up making drugs or toxic things that may defile us in the end. That is the reason why the author is pleading with the reader to always ask for guidance so that we stay within the specified limits of the Lord so that our relationship with Him stays a sound relationship. (Matthew 4:10) (NIV) shows that Satan is the god of worldly things, which we have to be very careful when we are pursuing worldly wealth not to be carried away.

Who Controls the World?

(Matthew 4:9) (NIV) Although Satan does not own the world, he tries by all means to deceive us by saying that he would make us have them if we bow to his will. If we are following the footsteps of Christ, we have to stay in prayer so that we will be able to resist some of the devil's temptations. The devil takes advantage only if we cannot realise these could be temptations from the devil.

Since we were promised the Holy Spirit to guide us, we must always pray for His guidance so that we know that this is a temptation and avoid it.

When the devil took Jesus to the top of the mountain, he offered the wealth of the world to Jesus which might mean that he is in control of the world or that he may be falsely using the wealth of the world to deceive the people and lead many astray. With His grace we are made to know that in the beginning dominion of the earth was given to Adam and Eve. With his falsehood the devil wanted to take away that dominion from man, but the Lord intervened, and on the cross and at the resurrection that falsehood was defeated, and now we have to claim back that dominion. Man is here as the ambassador of the heavenly kingdom, that is what should be enlightened to a man to claim his dominion. In Matthew 28:18-20 it is stated clearly that all authority is given unto Jesus from heaven and earth, and here at the great commission Jesus was transferring that power to us let not the devil take it away again. The Lord said, my people perish because of lack of knowledge, that means if we know that the devil was defeated, and all authority given back to us, we will not be led astray any more. Here and there, the devil is still misleading some, that is why at the great commission He said go to all corners of the world so that no one is left at the hands of the devil who comes in so many different ways that you may not realise it is the devil, this good news must be spread so that that no must be taken away from the Lord with the lies of the devil. There is a very thin line between knowing what is right or what is a temptation, that is why Jesus said stay in prayer so that the Holy Spirit may dwell in you so that he can warn you when some of these temptations come to you, be guided by the Holy Spirit.

Using his subordinates, (evil spirits), Satan controls the world, but we are warned in (Romans 12:2) (NIV) that as followers of Jesus we should not conform to the deeds of this world, if we were taken into the things of this world once we would see it and try to avoid it, but that they come gradually without us noticing it, by the time we realise we will have drifted very far, it is for us to look after ourselves the we should not indulge too much into worldly things because the devil controls most of the earthly things, so let us have some limits to them. Let us be transformed to the heavenly things, we must realise that we are living in a world that is evil, so we must not conform to that, but to stay pure. We must not lose focus that we are working towards eternal life. It is us who must be able to select between evil and righteous life. We must be conformed to God's way of doing things, because His ways will lead us to live a righteous life. If we work closely with the Lord, He will show us what we are gifted in so that we pursue them for the promotion of the heavenly kingdom on earth. We must not take worldly things as they are, we must be selective knowing which ones to take which may lead us to eternal life which is what we are all working for. (John 14:25-31) (NIV). Jesus on His farewell, He said those who love Him must be happy that He was going away because if He was on earth physically, He would not be in every part of the world at the same time. He said if I go, I will send you the Holy Spirit who would be with you everywhere every time. He will be your guide all the time so that you will not be taking wrong decisions. The Holy Spirit is the power that Jesus promised that you will receive power. Now that we have this power, we have to do the wonderful works of God. This Holy Spirit must transform the lives of believers to manifest all the good works of the heavenly kingdom through believers. Politically, the earthly kingdom is advancing its own interest, where it cannot succeed, it will use force to get its own wishes. Where it says, it is creating peace is where it creates more problems and more unrest. Wars are fought in the name of creating peace, yet it brings more hatred. The best way to have peace is to follow Jesus' example, and carry our cross and follow Him. After going through such pain of carrying His cross and he was exhausted of being bitten and the pain of the nails going through his palms and feet He died, and buried but on the third day He conquered death and rose from the dead, through the resurrection God set up a good example for us to follow. We seem to make a U-turn when it pains us and unable to carry our cross to the end. Let us ask the saviour to give us the courage not to be discouraged, but to persevere until we reach that destination that we are aiming for.

30

At the end of Time

Christ will come from Heaven with the Power and Authority from God

(Matthew 28:18) (NIV) When Jesus came to His disciples after His resurrection Hie told them of the power that had been given to Him for both heaven and earth. He was telling them that He was imparting that power to them The reason for Him telling them that was, He was going to impart that power to them, and instructed them to carry on with his mission Then Jesus came to them and said, "all authority in heaven and on earth has been given to me." Jesus has imparted this authority on us to take this authority seriously using it with guidance from Him, because He is not just sending us, but made a promise that He would be with us. Let us have no fear as if we are doing it alone. We should make note how powerful Jesus' words are, because when Jesus was still with them, they were going to the Jews only, but in this case, because Jesus has said it Himself, look at what is happening the gospel has gone all over the world, which means those words have got authority. We have no option but to do what He is telling us to do, let us obey his commandment, He will not let us go alone He will be with us. Jesus rose from the dead to new life and has put new life in us all, the life of authority and power. Let us heed those promises of Jesus, he promised in (Acts 1:8) (NIV)that you will receive power He also said it strongly that this Holy Spirit will be with us where ever we go, and whatever we do.

Jesus was right when He refused to be king of Israel as they looked forward for Him to do, if he had agreed, He was going to be confined to one area of the world, but now He is king of the whole world. Let us serve Him faithfully and loyally, and as He is with us, we are going to change the world. The author is pleading with the reader that we are not alone but He is with us, let us go on and do His will.

The Kingship of Jesus is not of this World

(John 18:36) (NIV) When Jesus was being arrested, He would have used His powers to resist that, but He never resisted, which is a clear sign that His kingdom is not of this world. When Jesus was being asked by Pilate, His reply must open our spiritual eyes for us to be able to know who we are following and this should make our faith go deeper, because we now know who we are following. When we follow Him, we will not about the earthly kingdom knowing that we are in the heavenly kingdom. Even to this day, we have to keep on asking the Lord to open our Spiritual eyes because people still want Jesus to intervene in matters of this world politically, He still helps us to know that He came specifically for our souls. (John 6:15) (NIV) We have to keep on asking to be opened our spiritual eyes because according to Jesus' mission on earth we may be moving in parallel with the reality. They had stayed very long with Jesus but according to how they presented their accusations to Pilate, they were putting a different case altogether, so they had lost all His purpose and were perusing a different issue altogether. They were accusing Him with earthly accusations Jesus answering with the reality which they failed to grasp, when are we going to know the reality, although we may not be doing as the Pharisees and the Romans did but still, we may not have the reality of Him which we must keep on searching for and asking Him to help us if we want to be in that kingdom which we seem to be pursuing but without knowing the real truth.

The kingdom of this world follows and does things in a worldly manner. Jesus does His things according divine nature, so the worldly things will differ and are contradictory.

Jesus is asking us to be truthful like He is truthful and nothing else but to walk in His footsteps and be like Him so that we will qualify to be in the Trinity. Even though Jesus tried to explain it to us about the Spirituality of His kingdom, it appears these two kingdoms are still being mixed up. Jesus is asking us to come out of this world, by what we accept as the truth, He reveals everything in His word what are we accepting as the truth ourselves today? We are in this world but we are not of this world which, means what we do sometimes will conflict with the things of this world. Jesus derives His power from heaven, so when we follow Him, it means we must draw our power from spiritual realms, in order to be His true followers. What we do should not conform to the things of this world, we must be transformed from inside and the world must see that we transformed and we are following things that are not of this world, all what we do must be accepted in the eyes of God. We must try to avoid the lust of the world, the lust of the eyes and sometimes we take pride in some achievements in life and forget to give glory to Him who enables us to achieve that.,, live the best of your life by obeying God and doing the things that please Him and not the things that please this world for us to be good followers of Jesus we must change even the way we think we must be thinking only of the things that please God. The kingdom of God is the kingdom of righteousness, of love, peace and of the Holy Spirit. If you are living in the kingdom of God means you are living under the kingship of God, under His authority and His command, which if we are under His authority, we have to pay our allegiance to Him and our obedience to Him If we are living under His authority, His promise to us is that He will never leave us or forsake us His promise is we should not turn to any other gods for help or to pay any allegiance to them. The church helps the by spreading the word of God and to preach the gospel values to the people to stay in the word of God. In order to build the kingdom of God here on earth, we must stay righteously to be always happy and to be positive in all what we do, knowing that we are to promote the kingdom of God on earth always keep in touch through prayer We must show that we understood what we were taught by trying to live a perfect life that pleases God all the time this may be good because by our deeds we may get many people to know Christ, this will make them know the true God.

31

Christ will Take Over the Governments of the Earth

I n the end, Jesus will establish His authority on earth and established His rule on earth, so that mean that everyone must submit to that authority. (Revelation 11:15) (NIV) We are given time to repent and turn to Him before it is too late, there will be no excuse or to ask for more time yet this is the time to reflect, repent and confess all our sins, there will be no excuse because we were given enough time because He is sending His messengers daily to alert us of the time to come. The seventh trumpet will be sounded to announce the arrival of the king. The revelation is that God is to reign on earth. The scriptures that were locked up will be brought to the view of all the people. All the believers will say thank you Lord you have taken over power, because your rule is just and fair to everyone. We give thanks Lord Almighty, the one who was, is there, and is to come because you have taken your great power and reign. His judgement is no longer negotiable, but complete destruction to the unholy. That mean the Godly kingdom has taken control, and there is no escape of the evil ones. (Revelations 9:20-21) Yet before the destruction, the Lord did not want to take us unawares so He gives us enough warnings where He sees fit those warnings should be given.

The problem we face is that the governments of this world are so emersed in power that they forget that there is someone more powerful than them. This government which more powerful does its things according to plan. Its plan is not to please anybody, but to do things that are good for everyone, our kingdoms must be obedient to the one that is above all other governments, sometimes we do what pleases us not what pleases Him who has got all the powers. The Lord did His part because in sending preachers to forewarn the people before it happens. People seem to want to see miracles, or even to want to see a preacher who comes from heaven, but then, the Son of Man came and they even did not believe Him but nailed Him to the cross. Sometimes we wonder when we see plagues happening, they are prewarning to us to repent. People are hard hearted that they do not heed all these warnings. One thing bad with temptation is that it does not come with a bang but comes bit by bit until you become comfortable in the sinning habits that you will not want to change from that habit. That is the reason why we are kept on being reminded to keep on asking in prayer to say, lead us not into temptation because once we entertain the temptation it becomes a sin and becomes difficult to eradicate. We must confess our sins before it is too late, because there will come a time when it will be difficult to confess, because sin will be rooted in you.

(James 1:15) (NIV) we must not entertain those that we think are small sins who are we to classify them as small or big, we must classify them all as sins and stop entertaining them. In most cases we make excuses not wanting to admit, where ever we go wrong we want to put the blame on others not me, I am right it is the other person. It is a mark of good Christianity to accept responsibility and confess whatever wrong you have done, this will make you keep away from such wrong doings and do the right thing in future and save yourself from committing so dirty things again, try to avoid anything that can be avoided.

When He establishes that kingdom, it will be a kingdom of justice, and fair to everyone who stay a perfect life, and will deserve it. It is interesting to note that all what we are crying for will one day come to an end when Christ Himself will establish His kingdom which we are praying for day and night, (Revelation 17-22) (NIV) We are all crying for the mis rule of the governments of this world but we have words of relief, for His time is not our time, this is His final plan for the redemption of His children what we must pray for is not to lose heart because the time seems to be a long time, but He fulfils His promise. We must always be praying for the resurrection of our souls which we know we have been promise by His resurrection, so He promises us the things He did Himself. We are working towards our goal of the end time and that coming day, but the devil is trying by all means to get us off track, so we have to be vigilant. With the Lord on our side, we will always defeat them and celebrate together when He comes. The heavenly warrior will defeat the beast for us and we will rejoice in Him.

The Bible must be handled with care and great respect knowing that it was inspired by God for it to be made because God wanted His word to be known by His people. He avoided telling us the time of His second coming knowing that we were going to be complacent. His word is for us to stay alert for anytime He might come, this should be good news to those who are staying in faith. If He was to appear today, are we ready to receive Him and look at Him face to face? Our request is, come Jesus, but keep us faithful and pure so that you find us ready. Amen.

Printed in the United States
by Baker & Taylor Publisher Services